COLBY'S BOOK

of the

AMERICAN PIT BULL TERRIER

Louis B. Colby
with Diane Jessup

TS-246

© 1997 by T.F.H. Publications, Inc.

Distributed in the UNITED STATES to the Pet Trade by T.F.H. Publications, Inc., One T.F.H. Plaza, Neptune City, NJ 07753; distributed in the UNITED STATES to the Bookstore and Library Trade by National Book Network, Inc. 4720 Boston Way, Lanham MD 20706; in CANADA to the Pet Trade by H & L Pet Supplies Inc., 27 Kingston Crescent, Kitchener, Ontario N2B 2T6; Rolf C. Hagen Inc., 3225 Sartelon St. Laurent-Montreal Quebec H4R 1E8; in CANADA to the Book Trade by Vanwell Publishing Ltd., 1 Northrup Crescent, St. Catharines, Ontario L2M 6P5 ; in ENGLAND by T.F.H. Publications, PO Box 15, Waterlooville PO7 6BQ; in AUSTRALIA AND THE SOUTH PACIFIC by T.F.H. (Australia), Pty. Ltd., Box 149, Brookvale 2100 N.S.W., Australia; in NEW ZEALAND by Brooklands Aquarium Ltd. 5 McGiven Drive, New Plymouth, RD1 New Zealand; in Japan by T.F.H. Publications, Japan—Jiro Tsuda, 10-12-3 Ohjidai, Sakura, Chiba 285, Japan; in SOUTH AFRICA by Lopis (Pty) Ltd., P.O. Box 39127, Booysens, 2016, Johannesburg, South Africa. Published by T.F.H. Publications, Inc.

MANUFACTURED IN THE
UNITED STATES OF AMERICA
BY T.F.H. PUBLICATIONS, INC.

"That island of England breeds
very valiant creatures."
                    Shakespeare

My father, John P. Colby picutred with the author Louis and Goldie in October 1922.

Colby's Book of the

DEDICATION

This book is dedicated to my father,
John P. Colby (Jan 1875 — Jan 1941)
whose name has been synonymous with the
American Pit Bull Terrier for over 100 years.

Louis with a five-week old puppy from Colby's Zorro out of Colby's Bonnie. Photo taken September 1993.

CONTENTS

PREFACE

The purpose of this book is to record for the future fanciers and friends of the breed what it was really like in the world of the American Pit Bull Terrier. Nothing has been added or avoided—nor has any facet been amplified.

After more than one hundred years of being hailed as the greatest breed of all dogdom by people from all walks of life, nothing has been maligned as the American Pit Bull Terrier in the last two decades. The media has projected them as dangerous and unfit companions, particularly for children. Yet, I am the father of nine children who grew up with these dogs (several hundred of them) and there has never been an incident of aggression toward them or their friends. Most of my children "cut their teeth" chewing on puppies' and dogs' tails and ears. You could count on one hand the number of ill-mannered dogs we have had to put to sleep over the years. We *do not* expect any reader of this book to become interested in dog fighting—we *do* expect him, however, to come away with a greater appreciation for the breed.

Louis Colby
Newburyport, MA

INTRODUCTION

Vince Gill, one of our leading country singers, has a song out entitled "There's No Future In The Past," which in a few words describes the present situation of the American Pit Bull Terrier.

Since the passage of the Animal Welfare Act of 1976, the sport of dog fighting, while always illegal in this country, has diminished considerably. The days of issuing open challenges in print, or holding matches that drew many spectators, have ended. The heyday for the sport was roughly 1850–1950.

During his lifetime, John P. Colby bred and sold more Pit Bull Terriers than any other man, about 5,000 dogs. Letters from some of the leading dog men of all time are contained herein, as well as some documents to show proof of "the way it was." The names, dates, places are all actual—and *I have avoided naming any living person*, but have included the above-mentioned facts for their historical value.

CO-AUTHOR'S NOTE

The decision to assist Mr. Colby with this book presented me with a dilemma. While I was very honored to be asked to assist with such an important project, I was also repelled by the thought that anything I would do could possibly glamorize the fighting of dogs as it exists today. I am a humane officer by profession. I am an expert witness on court cases pertaining to illegal dog and cock fighting. And I am unalterably opposed to the matching of dogs. Mr. Colby understood all this and was sympathetic to my viewpoint. I like to think he honored me by asking me to assist him with this because, animal control officer or not, he could sense with me the survival and respect of the game cock and dog are number one. The history of the fighting animals is what it is, like it or not. And to deny these gallant animals their proper place in history would be wrong.

I first met Mr. Colby when my Pit Bulldog Dread and I were back in Massachusetts filming *The Good Son.* I had a black brindle Colby bitch at the time which was the epitome of the perfect Pit Bull, and I wanted to meet the man and the dogs who had produced her. Having met many dog and cock fighters before, and seen the type of people they were, I was a little wary of what I would find. I needn't have been.

Louis Colby is in a class all his own. To most accurately describe him you would say he is "of the old school." He has all the traits of the Pit Bull—quiet courage, courtesy, pride, honesty (and good looks!). He has an amazing memory—really it's startling—and can rattle off the birth dates of dogs dead 75 years like he was speaking of a favorite dog born two years ago. What endeared him to me the most was the care he took of his animals. I was there in the winter and his fowl were all cozy in coops covered in clear plastic to break the bitter wind. His dogs were comfortable in insulated dog houses stuffed with straw and had all-important door flaps. His respect for his animals shows in his care of them.

I understand the concept of gameness, and I, like most people, admire it. But I do not confine my definition of gameness to a dog's ability to beat up another dog; I define it as willingness to complete a task no matter how tired, discouraged or hurt it is. To say that a gamecock or Pit Bull "enjoys" fighting is to blind yourself to the fact that fighting is painful and stressful and not designed to be enjoyed. Dogs and cocks have been genetically engineered over thousands of years to ignore the laws of nature and to seek out and fatally harm their own kind. So it is ridiculous to say the animals are "doing what's natural for them." But mankind admires the fighter (more specifically the winner) and, admittedly, there is not much to admire about a quitter. And that is what draws people to the game animals. Some of the greatest thrills of my life have included watching my little Colby bitch out-pull larger Huskies at weight pulls, or Annette Cheeks' outstanding red-nosed bitch being the only dog (let alone a little bitch) to knock down the "bad guy" at the Schutzhund nationals; something the big male Rottweilers, Malinois and German Shepherds couldn't do. The Pit Bull stands alone as a dog breed—its heart stands out whatever the task it is asked to do. And that is gameness, and that is what makes the breed unique.

Even though a very small percentage of Pit Bulls have ever been matched, I think, right or wrong, it is folly to deny the place dog fighting has had in the history and development of the breed. And it is equally folly to deny that almost every Pit Bull owner feels a secret pride in their little dog's prowess and ability to take care of themselves. I, myself, smile a little smile when some large, aggressive, obnoxious dog (generally owned by an equally aggressive, obnoxious owner) lunges and snarls at my little Pit Bulls. My dogs calmly ignore the empty threat, and go about their business, very secure in themselves. They *know* that they can take care of themselves, and they don't feel compelled to meet every idle threat. And that is why I like the breed—they don't make threats and they don't waste time on pointless aggression. But as happy and carefree as they are, they should not be challenged with impunity.

As I wrap up the last bit of work on this book I am glad I did agree to work on it. Even though I cannot agree with breeding or training dogs to be antisocial to their own kind (for the world is getting smaller, and we all must get along), I do acknowledge the part that men like J. P. Colby and his son Louis played in the development of the dogs I love. It would be less than honest to say that their stewardship of the breed over the past 100 years was excellent, and we all owe them a debt of gratitude for passing on such excellent dogs for the next generation.

Louis Colby and I are quite different. Yet for one afternoon, on the day we met, the differences fell away and we talked of our admiration for the game birds and dogs. On that cold January day I learned that maybe, years ago, the matching of dogs really was no worse than hunting, dog racing, or rodeo. And maybe Louis learned that it is possible to be a humane officer, and opposed to fighting animals for sport, and still be obsessed with the preservation of the game cock and dog. And maybe that is the magic of the game fowl and Pit Bull.

Diane Jessup

THE COLBY FAMILY

One of the true treasures of the British Isles has been its dogs. From that isolated grouping of islands has come some of the world's most beloved breeds such as the Beagle; Foxhound; the Irish, English and Gordon Setters; the Springer and Cocker Spaniels; the show Collie and the clever working Border Collie. With the exception of the Schnauzers, every type of terrier the world knows today was developed in the United Kingdom. Yet the breed most commonly associated with the British Isles, and indeed, the breed that has come to symbolize British (and Irish) courage, pride, and love of a good scrape is the fighting Bulldog known today as the American Pit Bull Terrier.

There is a common misconception that the breed registered by show clubs as "Bulldog" today is the working Bulldog of the past, when in fact nothing could be further from the truth. The show Bulldog is a recently developed show breed based on a written standard. This written standard has no basis in working dog physiology, but rather was the

John Pritchard Colby, here a young man at the turn of the century. He is shown with "red and white" Paddy.

Colby's Book of the

Florence Fuller Colby poses with her dog Dixie.

fanciful idea of a group of show enthusiasts who took it upon themselves to determine the proper form of a bull-baiting dog. They seemed not to care that dogs had been catching and baiting bulls for centuries, and that the breed with a functional form for this already existed. This breed was depicted in pictures such as the much-reproduced 1809 engraving entitled *Wasp, Child and Billy*, and is reputed to show what the true working Bulldog appeared like. The dogs depicted in this engraving are about 50 pounds, stand on long straight legs, have rose ears and a fine, thin tail. These dogs are indistinguishable from modern-day American Pit Bull Terriers.

Another line drawing from 1887 shows "John Bull," the English version of America's "Uncle Sam," with his companion—and the symbol of England as well—the Pit Bulldog. This dog, too, shows long straight legs and a normal muzzle. This type of working Bulldog had survived for centuries as a butcher's dog, guardian, and baiting animal. This Bulldog survives today in the strains of the Pit Bull and Staffordshire dogs. Some of the larger strains of Pit Bull Terrier have recently been inbred to create a breed called the American Bulldog, which is reputed to be a direct descendant of the working Bulldog, but which is in fact larger and heavier in build than ever was the true working Bulldog. Other strains of Pit Bull Terrier have been bred to small game terriers, which developed into tiny, lightly built dogs. This is the reason why the purebred Pit Bull Terrier of today can vary so greatly in appearance.

A very nice description of a true working Bulldog fancier's feelings concerning the public's misconception of the newly created show breed Bulldog as the true British Bulldog was printed in a pamphlet published in 1872.

> *At every dog show at Curzon Hall, when delicate young ladies and benighted young gentlemen approach the row of ugly, pug-nosed, big-headed, affectionate, slobbering brutes at the end of the gallery, just over the stage, we hear the cry "Oh! here are the fighting dogs," and etiquette bids us suffer in silence.*

There will always be discussion on just how much true Bulldog blood remains in today's dogs. Obviously there was some terrier blood crossed in—how else to reconcile with 19-pound fighting dogs? Whatever the percentage of Bulldog to terrier, there are dogs in today's breed that show marked tendencies toward both families.

The Pit Bull thrived in England, Ireland, Wales, and Scotland. When immigration from the United Kingdom began, the famous fighting dogs came along as well. No country in the world can claim dogs that excel in courage and grit like the United Kingdom; indeed many of the world's fighting type dogs, such as the Presa Canario, Cane Corso, Dogo Argentino, Dogue de Bordeaux, and Tosa owe what valor they have to the blood of the British fighting dogs that sailed the world over with their Empire-building masters. In America the dogs found use as watchdogs for pioneers and homesteaders, as stock dogs and as a sport dogs for gamblers.

Colby's Book of the

In America, before the turn of the century, there was a young boy growing up in the port town of Newburyport, Massachusetts, who was destined to have his "name...so closely associated with Pit Bulldogs that it's a common belief they are descended solely from his line of dogs." (*The Pit Bull: Fact and Fable*). This boy was John Pritchard Colby, and he was to have perhaps the largest single impact on the fighting Pit Bull Terrier in America as any one person can claim.

J.P. Colby in a tin-type photo taken in 1883 when he was eight years old–about the time he owned his first Pit Bull Terrier.

John P. Colby (J.P.) was born January 15, 1875. Many dog books claim he was Irish, but this is due more to misinformation concerning his special love for Irish-bred dogs then to the reality of his lineage. He was in fact Welsh, and his paternal grandfather came directly to America from Wales. His father's people had settled in Newburyport during the 1700s and most of the men in the family went to sea.

Newburyport was an active port town, and the clipper trade was still flourishing when J.P.'s father, Joseph Lunt Colby VI, was a young man plying his trade as ship's carpenter. Joseph L. was ship's carpenter aboard the clipper "Gem of the Ocean." His brother-in-law, Captain John Pritchard, was in command. The Gem was a dainty, speedy, medium-sized ship (152'x31'x20'), built in 1852 by Haden and Cudworth at Medford, Massachusetts.

The Gem's maiden run was to San Francisco via Cape Horn, and she arrived February 2, 1853, making the passage in 120 days. The Gem traveled extensively over the next few years, going to Manila, Austria, India, and Hong Kong, arriving back in San Francisco on May 26, 1867. Captain Pritchard then took her to Alaska for a load of ice. His wife Abbie Colby Pritchard became the first person to carry the American flag into Alaska after the U.S. purchased it from Russia.

The Gem was purchased by a Pacific company for $18,000 in gold and stayed on the West Coast. Joseph L. came back to Massachusetts, but found work in Springfield, on the west side of the state, and was again absent from home for long periods of time. His son, John Pritchard, growing up with his mother and sister, sought out the local men who told him exciting tales of the courageous fighting cocks and dogs of their homelands.

Newburyport was a real haven for game dogs and fowl. The history of the town is intertwined with the development of these animals. Many of the most famous strains of dog and fowl were developed right in town, such as the Colby dogs and the Tracy Pyle game fowl. Nathaniel Tracy's (1751-1796) father, Patrick Tracy, had emigrated from Ireland to Newburyport in 1735. In 1771 he erected an elegant brick mansion (now the public library on State Street) for his eldest son, Nathaniel. Nathaniel earned local fame by fitting out and operating a fleet of 24 ships, carrying 2,800 men, that carried out "privateering" of legalized piracy against English ships. These vessels captured 120 enemy ships with cargo valued at four million dollars. He was considered a great patriot, but unfortunately he ran into financial problems and died quite young. The Tracy family is credited with bringing the Irish Pyle chickens from Ireland to America, in fact, right into Newburyport. The descendants of these same birds can be found at the Colby place to this day.

An example of an old-time Tracy Pyle cock. Most are a distinctive red and white coloring (Pyle), this one is primarily white. Photograph circa 1900.

While his father was away at sea, or later working across the state, young J.P. hung around the blacksmith's shops and in the inns where the old Irish and Englishmen met to talk about the unique qualities of their fighting animals. One of J.P.'s favorites was a blacksmith named Ed Donahue who kept his fighting dogs at his shop on Inn Street. Another was John Burham, a Scotsman, who had a strain of brown/red fowl that were reputed to take their death in the pit as young as seven months of age.

The Boston area was a haven for the Irish. As J.P.'s interest in the dogs and chickens grew it was not difficult for him to have access to some of the best stock in the world. The only place in the world where true fighting animals were bred was in the

J.P. Colby and "friend," circa 1900, out for a Sunday afternoon drive in his fancy buggy, the first with pneumatic tires in Newburyport.

United Kingdom, and from the UK they came with the immigrants. Soon some of the UK's finest dogs (and cocks) resided in America, and the material was available to develop an excellent strain of dogs. The breed also began to grow in popularity—not just among fighters, but among families who came to know the breed's gentle and loyal nature with people. It was an age when dash, daring and courage were much admired, and the breed epitomized those qualities.

In the words of his son Louis, "J.P. never worked five minutes for any man." He began breeding game fowl and dogs and was successful enough to be able to support himself with them. Later he was able to support himself, a wife and seven children right through the Great Depression.

J.P. never cared to drive an automobile, instead he traveled around Newburyport on a fancy rubber-wheeled cart pulled by "Kitty" the standardbred mare. Kitty was eight years old when J.P. bought her, and worked steadily and sturdily up until the time of her death, thirty years later.

On one such drive J.P. noticed a pretty new woman in town. She was Florence Fuller, of Richmond, Maine, and she had followed her brother to Newburyport looking for work. She was working

Louis Colby says of this picture: "Except for J.P. here are some of the Boston Irish Gang. All good dog men and gentlemen as well." Left to right: Tom Byron, racing pigeon and Pit Bull fancier who once owned a red male litter brother to Colby's Primo; J.P. Colby; Patsy Reardon, who was head of the Boston department of public works and an avid fan of the Pit Bull; and Henry Collagan, one of J.P.'s closest friends for over 50 years.

Colby's Book of the

as a telephone operator when she caught the eye of J.P. as he rode down the road in his fancy cart, and after a time she became Mrs. Florence Fuller Colby.

J.P. was an intensely proud man, a fact that probably drew him to the proud little English and Irish dogs. His son Louis describes his father as a man who "wouldn't go to town to buy dog meat unless he put on a clean shirt and a bowtie first." Louis smiles remembering how, during the Great Depression, people around Newburyport thought that J.P. had money because of his appearance and the clothes he wore. In reality, says Louis, he often didn't have a dime in his pocket.

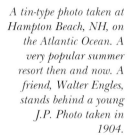

A tin-type photo taken at Hampton Beach, NH, on the Atlantic Ocean. A very popular summer resort then and now. A friend, Walter Engles, stands behind a young J.P. Photo taken in 1904.

J.P. and Florence raised five boys, John Jr., Joseph VII, Louis B., Alexander (Mike), and J. Richard, as well as two daughters, Marjorie and Helen. Louis remembers his father as a man who never smoked or drank, who would not allow a gun in the house, who never spanked the children and who took outstanding care of his animals. He was a family man, and his career offered plenty of time to be with the wife and kids. Most photographs of J.P. have a kid, a dog or both in the picture somewhere.

Though it is difficult for those who choose to keep dogs as companions to consider dog fighting as anything but cruel, to those who enjoy it, it is simply another form of animal sport, no crueler than other sports involving other animals, such as hunting, rodeo, or racing. Within the sport there are standards, even, of what is considered cruel or unsportsmanlike. For instance, Louis considers setting Pit Bulls on pigs or hogs to be less than humane because the pig is not a willing participant. Pig hunting and baiting, which is legal in most of the United States and which is finding favor with a small group of Pit Bull and American Bulldog owners, would have been considered cruel and pointless to turn-of-the-century breeders, who strove to produce animals which would fight willingly against *equally* willing opponents. J.P. considered matching dogs of unequal weight, or unconditioned dogs, to be cruel. It is beyond the scope of this book to discuss the ethical questions surrounding dog fighting. This book looks at the development of the Pit Bull breed, such as it was. The ideas and methods of the men that shaped it are of historical interest. The point is, J.P. himself did not consider the matching of dogs to be crueler than many other sports involving animals, and he attempted to make the testing of his fighting dogs as humane as possible, considering the circumstances.

J.P.'s work with the dogs took him to Boston at least once a week, where he kept a couple of big "try out" dogs named Callahan and Oklahoma upstairs in a livery stable. There were several dog men, known locally as the "Irish Boston Gang," who were involved in pit dogs in the Boston area. J.P. would ride the train the 40 miles in from Newburyport to look at new dogs and "talk shop" with the likes of Teddy Racine and Mike Redican. If a dog looked

Photo of a door from J.P.'s workshop, where he built the noiseless treadmills, mated dogs, etc. On this door, J.P. would post breedings of dogs in the early days when record-keeping was not the norm. It is multicolored from wiping out paint brushes on it, and it is also tinned-over on bottom where dogs had gnawed on it. This door is all that is left of the house at 19 Salem Street, which was located directly behind the family home and served as a kennel, stable for Kitty, and workshop. Louis still has this old door, which he salvaged when the building was sold and torn down.

Joseph Lunt Colby VI. Joe in a photo taken at about two years of age. This photo hangs in Louis Colby's home, as it did in the Colby homestead at 36 Franklin Street. Joe, second-eldest son of J.P., wrote his book on the breed in 1936 while operating a kennel in California. He left Newburyport at the age of 17 and moved to California, where he lived all his life.

good after a few minutes with Callahan and Oklahoma, J.P. would purchase the dog and head home. Louis recalls one story his father told him concerning a match that took place upstairs in the loft where Callahan and Oklahoma were kept. Just before the match was about to begin, J.P. looked out and saw a priest, in robes, coming toward the stable through a hole in the fence. "Oh-oh," he said, fearing interference, "we got trouble, here comes a priest." He was assured by the locals that this priest was a regular at frequented Boston-area dog fights. Later in the match when the local dog was down, somebody said "time to call the priest." The priest looked into the pit and declared dryly, "never mind the priest, it's time to call the undertaker."

The Irish-bred dogs were of particular interest to J.P.; he would talk to immigrants about their dogs, and even arrange work in America for men still in Ireland if they would bring a good dog or two with them. Once he purchased a dog, it would come home to him at the Colby house at 36 Franklin Street. Actually the dogs stayed in the house directly behind the Franklin Street address, in a house that faced Salem Street, which J.P. had bought for the express purpose of outfitting as a kennel, workshop, and stall for Kitty. That was certainly before the days of restrictive city zoning!

J.P. always kept a large number of dogs. Louis states that one reason for the success of the Colby line when compared to other lines is that his father always kept as many males as females, thus "never breeding himself into a corner." J.P. was able to do this by farming a great many dogs out, especially puppies, which he believed produced a better dog. Kennel-raised dogs were not as intelligent as dogs raised as family pets, and so he made many deals with surrounding families to raise his pups or keep a dog or two for him. Some would keep a pup for pay, others would do it in exchange for a puppy to keep as a pet. He kept copious notes; in fact J.P. was famous for his scrupulous record-keeping. A Colby pedigree could be trusted, it was (and still is) said. Pete Sparks, longtime pit dog breeder, stated in an article that appeared in *Sporting Dog Journal* in 1984, that just about every pedigree on a Pit Bull could be counted on being falsified, with the exception of the Colby dogs. An example of this record-keeping shows how a young pup, Colby's Jim, which was being sent off to be raised by a neighbor, was described in detail so as to be positively identified upon return. It was touches like this that made accurate record-keeping a trademark of J.P. Colby.

The description of Colby's Jim, as recorded by J.P. in his notebook, makes the Colby pedigrees the most respected in the fancy: "White stripe on face and fore head (white collar around neck) (white tip on tail) (four white feet) more white on left front leg than on right front leg—one little tiny brindle spot on right side of back of neck—has more white on left front side of muzzle than on right side."

It is interesting to note that it is a common misconception today that the Pit Bull is somehow unsafe as a child's dog. J.P. and Florence raised seven children in a home where children played in a yard filled with history's most famous fighting Pit Bull Terriers. Looking at a picture of himself

GAME FIGHTING DOGS
(BULL TERRIERS)

Containing the blood of John Galvin's "Turk," Teddy Racine's Danger" Charley Lloyd's "Pilot," Colby's "Tige" and "Pincher," Paddy Mitchell's dog "Paddy," Quigg's "Boxer," "Bob The Fool" Jimmy McDonald's Famous "Gas-House Dog," Moldy McCarthy's "Blind Dog," and the Imported Rafferty"

We have the nearest descendants of these Famous Dogs and the old time Boston dogs now living

It is easy enough to get good lookers and good fighters, But It Takes the Game Dog to Win

JOHN P. COLBY
36 FRANKLIN STREET

Newburyport, Mass.,_____192-

"PINCHER"
Newburyport's great fighting dog that never was beaten
Pincher killed or stopped over twenty dogs
and never met a dog that could stay with him forty minutes

J.P. Colby's letterhead from the 1920s.

sitting on the curb beside his father who is holding a pregnant bitch, Louis remarks, "I was rocked in the cradle to dogs barking." Of the seven children it was Louis who would take the most interest in the dogs.

John P. Jr., the eldest, went into the Navy in WWII and worked for the US Postal Service all his life. He never took much interest in dogs or fowl.

Joseph, according to brother Louis, never showed any real interest in dogs until he left home at 17 and moved to California. It was out there in Sacramento that he met men like John Fonsenca and realized he missed the dogs. He had his father send him dogs and began breeding his own Colby dogs. In 1936 he wrote a well-received booklet on the breed that is still selling well to this day.

The two girls, Marjorie and Helen, did not become involved in either the dogs or the chickens.

Alexander (Mike) settled back in Newburyport and made treadmills and bred some Colby dogs for a while.

J. Richard worked in the Postal Service after his return from the war and became interested in standardbred horses. He never kept Pit Bulls but still has standardbreds to this day.

American Pit Bull Terrier ——————————————— 23

Louis, on the other hand, was always intensely interested in both dogs and fowl. He tagged after his father as he cared for and conditioned his animals. He attended fights from his very earliest age. He was surrounded by Pit Bulls, racing pigeons and battle fowl from his birth, and during the course of his long life he has never lost interest in any of them.

When WWII came, Louis thought he would be placed in the K-9 Corps, but found himself instead in the Pigeon Corps, helping the government to develop a long-range pigeon capable of flying across seas, and also worked on ways to drop messenger pigeons out of flying aircrafts. Louis recalls that thousands of pigeons lost their lives before the military figured out that by putting a pigeon in a brown paper bag, then slitting the sides, the bird could work its way out while the bag dropped.

J.P. Colby died in 1941. At that time the family struggled to keep the breeding program in place, and it was finally Louis who stepped forward to maintain the breeding program his father had implemented years before. He has successfully maintained that line to the present day.

Louis' son Jack, a chemist whose line of work has taken him all over the world (from Hong Kong to Alaska), is now living with his family outside Dallas. He and his son Adam are breeding Colby dogs in Texas. Thus, Adam becomes the fourth generation of Colbys to be involved with the dogs.

Son Peter lives in Newton Junction, New Hampshire, and he too has a genuine interest in the dogs and has maintained a kennel of Colby dogs for the past twenty or so years.

Son Paul now carries on the tradition of making the treadmills. He is the third generation to build these carpet mills. Louis' youngest son, Scott, still lives at home so he has the Colby dogs at his elbow. He is full-time into the standardbred Trotters and Pacers, and also owns two teams of heavy draft horses. He keeps a Colby dog as a watchdog in the stable he shares with my brother Dick.

Happily, there are avid fans of the bloodline all over the world now, and it appears that this respected and famous line of dogs will be preserved well in to the future, perhaps forever.

THE FOUNDATION

THE PRIDE OF ENGLAND AND IRELAND COMES TO AMERICA

Among the admirers of the Pit Bull, the Colby family of dogs have obtained worldwide recognition not only for their abilities but also for the sheer duration of the line, which has prospered for over 100 years. No other line of dogs could have endured so long under the harsh conditions in which this breed was forged, unless based on a very sound foundation. The dogs upon which J.P. based his line were animals brought from England, Ireland, and Wales to America by immigrants and the occasional dog importer who was assured of finding a market for quality fighting dogs, particularly around the Boston area. There are stories of promising-looking immigrants' dogs' being stolen right at the docks by the Boston dog-fighting gang. The mother of "Sweeney's Fly" (a.k.a. "The Gas House Bitch"), a white bitch, was said to have been stolen in this manner and thus introduced into the bloodline of many famous dogs.

The Colby line was based on the gamest fighting dogs of that time. Most of the dogs died in the pit, still trying to cross to their opponent, or shortly after the battle, from injuries sustained while fighting. This was the kind of genetic material that J.P. needed, and he found it in the English and Irish dogs. J.P. was of Welsh descent, yet he admired the Irish dogs the most, and kept a constant eye out for newly arrived Irish dogs. He would meet and talk to new immigrants who had brought their dogs along, always looking for a quality dog that he could purchase. He did not pick dogs up randomly—he had a very specific goal in mind. The dogs that were the foundation of the Colby line were all celebrated dogs, and worthy of respect for their gameness and courage, regardless of whether you approve of the use to which men put them.

JOHN GALVIN'S TURK (a.k.a. FARMER'S TURK)

Turk lived around 1891 and was the son of Galvin's Prince (brother to Galvin's Pup) out of Conner's White Bitch. Galvin's Prince was sired by Woburn Bucky and his dam, Jumbo, who was out of Burk's Tanner and Sweeney's Fly, two dogs of fighting fame. Turk was a white dog with lemon patches over his eyes and on his hips. On December 6, 1891 John Galvin, who operated a barroom in Boston, matched his dog against Con Feeley's Jim. The fight was one of the longest on record, with both dogs dying in the pit. The decision on who won this 4-hour 58-minute fight had never been clear, with both sides claiming fouls. Obviously neither dog was a "winner" or a "loser," as it was a tragic loss of two game dogs, and both dogs had refused to yield until every ounce of strength had gone from their bodies.

The Incredible Galvin's Pup, a serious-looking little dog that is reported to have won nine fights "without ever making a turn." There is a story told of one of his fights when he was handled by James Boutelle, going against Gregory's Brindle, handled by Benjamin Miller. It is said that Miller, upon seeing Boutelle for the first time at the weigh-in, remarked to his friends, "I'll give him a lesson in dog fighting this morning." When the dogs were set against each other the next morning, there was a lesson learned, but perhaps not by Boutelle. Boutelle pried Pup off of Miller's dead dog after 2 hours 47 minutes. This fight took place on November 24, 1890.

TEDDY RACINE'S DANGER

This dog lived around 1895 and was killed in a fight with Quigg's Boxer. Danger had been punishing Boxer for over 40 minutes when he had an artery cut in his shoulder and weakened fast. Danger's handler decided to remove Danger from the pit, but it was too late, and the dog died.

Colby's Book of the

CHARLIE LLOYD'S PILOT

Born around 1878, Pilot was brought to America by a man called "Cockney" Charlie Lloyd of England. Lloyd brought two dogs with him on his last trip to America, Pilot and Paddy, of which he said, "Pilot is the best fighter, but Paddy is the gamest."

Pilot was bred by John Holden, of the Red Lion Inn, Park Street, Walsall, in England. His sire was Small's Billy, and he came from a long line of famous fighting dogs. Pilot was brindle and white, and most of his line weighed around 36 pounds. Pilot was fought at 27 pounds. Looking at the picture of Pilot, it is apparent that at that point in time the Pit Bull and the English "Staffordshire Bull" were one and the same thing.

Cockney Charlie Lloyd and his famous imported dog, Pilot. This dog won the famous Pilot–Crib fight of 1881. This picture has been in the Colby family for over 100 years.

Pilot became an American celebrity when Cockney Charlie accepted a challenge issued in the *Police Gazette* magazine by Louis Krieger of Louisville to fight his Crib dog for $1,000 a side. That was a considerable sum of money in 1881. This fight attracted considerable attention due to its being published in the *Police Gazette*, which was a widely read paper. The dogs met on a farm six miles outside of Louisville, Kentucky, on October 19, 1881. Pilot won over the 27 1/2-pound Crib in 1 hour 25 minutes. Crib attempted to jump the pit near the end of the fight, but was caught by the leg and dragged back in by Pilot.

Colby's Tige (1896), a dog that was extremely significant in the Colby breeding program, and indeed in the development of a great many Pit Bull Terriers. He died Sunday, September 30, 1906. He was a strikingly handsome brindle and white dog that went 35 pounds pit weight.

COLBY'S TIGE

Tige was bred by J.P. and whelped in 1896, sired by Colby's Paddy and out of Colby's Jennie. Tige became known as the best 35-pound dog in the area, which was quite a compliment since he lived in the very heart of dog-fighting country. He became a very well respected dog, and his fame was assured forever when he won a spectacular battle against a Connecticut dog named Dan Rose's Captain in 3 hours 27 minutes. Tige was bred to over 40 bitches and had a significant impact on the breed.

Louis Colby tells a story of Tige, involving his love for the water. Tige would often be taken by J.P. down to the Merrimack River, where it emptied into the harbor, and be allowed to swim. A group of "sports" in Boston had a Newfoundland dog that was a powerful swimmer, and upon which they would wager bets as to his swimming prowess. J.P. took Tige to Boston to challenge these men, wagering his Pit Bull could out-swim the Newfie for $500.00 a side. Tige is reported to have brought home the money.

Many prominent dog fighters were eager to obtain breeding from Tige, and in particular, Bill Lightner was obtaining a bitch from Colby, bred off Tige, to breed to his Masterson's Jack. J.P. bred Tige to his daughter Colby's Neitz, for the express purpose of sending the pick bitch to Lightner. J.P. himself picked the best of the litter for Lightner, a red-nosed bitch named Colby's Topsey.

Colby's Book of the

COLBY'S PINCHER

Colby's Pincher, "Newburyport's Famous Fighting Dog," was born December 31, 1896, and was a large white and dark spotted dog that weighed 75 pounds normally, and was fought at 56 pounds. Pincher's sire was White's Teddy, and his dam, Colby's Pansy, was sired by Teddy Racine's Sam, the dog that beat the famous Smuggler in 1 hour 30 minutes, and also beat a son of Galvin's Pup. Colby's Pansy herself was a winner of three fights. Pincher was a big, rough dog, and was reported to have stopped 24 dogs in his career, none of them able to fight him for over 40 minutes. Pincher was as great a sire as he was a fighter, and he sired Colby's Bunch. Pincher's grandsire was Cockney Charlie Lloyd's Pilot.

Says Louis Colby of this dog: "When you're looking at this picture of Pincher, you're looking at the greatest dog of all times. First let's back up and see if you would agree that the Pit Bull dog is the greatest of breeds. If you agree on that then it would be a Pit Bull that would be the greatest dog of all time, and Pincher surely would fit that description.

"He had the most noble look on his face—a look of honesty and depth. He too had the advantage of maturing slowly, as an old man named Parker who had a small farm on the outskirts of Newburyport took Pincher to raise him as a pup. And every six months or so my father would go visit Parker and see how Pincher was doing. And he would ask Parker, 'Has Pincher started any fights yet?' and Parker would say no. So along about when Pincher was

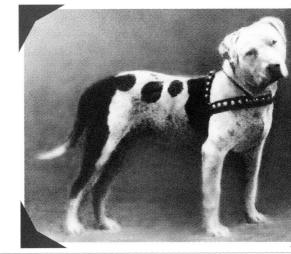

J.P. Colby's Pincher (whelped 1896). He weighed 72 pounds when not trimmed down for fighting. "Newburyport's Famous Fighting Dog," and Louis Colby's choice for "the greatest dog that ever lived."

about three years old, J.P. goes up there one day to visit and Parker says 'Well I guess you gotta take old Pincher back because he got a hold of a dog the other day and the other dog running off dragged him through a barbed wire fence and cut up his side.' So J.P. says 'Ok, I'll bring you up another pup and take Pincher back.' So you see, by running at large like that for three years a dog just develops that much more and knows that much more. (Author's note: please remember that this discussion concerns allowing dogs to run loose at the turn of the century—not at the present time!)

"So anyway that is in Pincher's early life. But in all the years my father had him, using him as a catch weight dog or as a try-out dog, nothing could ever stay with Pincher. He was a terrific punisher. 'Course he was big enough, being a catch weight dog—I would venture to say that Pincher could have licked any dog that ever lived. Regardless of weights, because he was a big dog too.

"You're looking at what might well be the greatest dog of all time. There have been great stories about Kager, Buddy, Webster's Joker, Twister, but Pincher could have licked them all. He was big enough and good enough to do it. Yet a little child could bite on his ear, or grab his tail or try and ride him, and he would just turn around and try to lick his face."

PADDY MITCHELL'S PADDY

This dog was sired by Cockney Charlie Lloyd's Pilot out of Cockney Charlie Lloyd's Pansy.

QUIGG'S BOXER

Boxer was whelped in 1893 and died in the pit in 1896. He was bred by Patrick Hanley and owned by Charles Quigg. He was sired by Malone's Boxer whose dam was Henley's Minnie. Minnie was sired by O'Neill's Frank whose dam was Gallivan's Sal. Gallivan's Sal was sired by McCafferty's Imported Mouldy.

Boxer was the winner of two great battles fought in Boston. He beat Teddy Racine's Danger in a controversial fight in 1896. Boxer died after winning a fight with Nagle's Prince. Boxer fought at 33 pounds.

Old Spring contained the blood of John Galvin's Turk, Colby's Tige and Quigg's Boxer. He won in 3 hours 15 minutes over Gilligen's Crib at Boxford, MA in April 1897.

BOB THE FOOL (a.k.a. GALLIGAN'S BOB OR MCGOUGH'S BOB)

It is not known if Bob the Fool ever fought a money match, but he has become very famous as the producer of an entire strain of good dogs. Bob and McDonald's Grip are the two dogs referred to the most often as having the largest impact on the development of the breed at the turn of the century. Bob was sired by Jack Burke's Spring, a 31-pound dog that won fame for winning nine fights in one year alone. Spring was sired by Blind Buck, who in turn was sired by Imported Turk. On his dam's side he traces back to a bitch called BobTail who was sired by Imported Bowler and out of Morrow's Fly.

JOHNNY MCDONALD'S GAS HOUSE DOG (a.k.a. MCDONALD'S GRIP)

This famous and imported dog was born around 1870. He was sired by the Imported Middleton Dog out of Sweeney's Fly (a.k.a. The Gas House Bitch) whose mother was the white dog stolen from Irish immigrants at a Boston dock. Grip was a 29-pound brindle and white who reportedly killed nine dogs. He is probably best remembered throughout history for fighting a famous battle with Sheridan's Blind Dog that ended in a draw at the end of three hours. McDonald's Grip is immortalized in the story *White Monarch and the Gas House Pup*, which tells the fictional story of the battle between Grip and a show-type Bull dog.

MOULDY MCCARTHY'S BLIND DOG

This dog, known as Pete, lived 20 years after the Blind Dog who fought McDonald's Grip to a draw. There is some question as to the breeding of this dog, the owner stating he bred the dog, but most everyone else agreeing that the dog was imported. This dog's fame was won when he crawled across the pit toward his opponent after the crowd had determined him to be dead.

"TURK," CHAMPION FIGHTING CANINE OF CHICAGO.

WINNER OF THE RECENT GREAT BATTLE OF 4 HOURS AND 58 MINUTES, AGAINST CON FEELEY'S "JIM."

CHAMPION CANINE "TURK."

[With Portrait.]

The Farmer Brothers, of 489 W. Lake street, Chicago, writing to the POLICE NEWS, say: "We forward you the picture of 'Turk,' owned formerly by John Galvin, of Boston. 'Turk's' great winning fight here was for $400 a side. He fought Coney Feeley's dog 'Jim.' The fight lasted for 4 hours and 58 minutes, and $2000 changed hands. The gate receipts were $600."

Two old cuttings showing dogs that lived around 1890. Taken from the Police Gazette. *Turk's battle took place at Niles Center, IL, on December 6, 1861 and was known as "the longest fight on record."*

IMPORTED RAFFERTY

This little 14-pounder fought over a dozen battles with none lasting over 40 minutes. This dog had a strong desire to kill, and would allow himself to go under a dog in order to get his desired throat hold. When Rafferty arrived in America he was one of a shipment of five dogs. He was reputed to be the best dog in England, and was valued at 100 pounds. He was sold because no matches could be found for

CHAMPION "BEN."

A 37-POUND FIGHTING CANINE, OF ST. PAUL,
MINN., CHAMPION OF THE NORTHWEST.

CHAMPION "BEN."

A 37-Pound Fighting Dog of St. Paul, Minn., Challenger of the Northwest.

[With Portrait from Photograph.]

Champion Ben is a 37-pound fighting dog owned by G. W. Wells, of St. Paul, Minn. He has never been defeated, and was the winner of the recent fight in Minneapolis. He has whipped Penny, 47 pounds, of Portland, Ore., in 37 minutes; stopped Whirlwind Jack, Jan. 1, 1891, in 1 hour 45 minutes; stopped Blair's dog, Sullivan, Jr., 45 pounds, out of Champion Sullivan, in 13 minutes; stopped William Hickey's dog, Spot, 64 pounds, in 21 minutes, and is now ready to fight any dog in the Northwest at 37 pounds for $100 to $500 at any time. Ben is a brindle, and a beauty, and if any one thinks he is a quitter he ll find dog and money at G. W. Wells', 82 East reet, St. Paul, Minn.

him. When the dog arrived the English owner wrote to say that he had found a match, and desired to buy the dog back. Rafferty's new owner, Jack Burke, would not give him up, and Rafferty became a house dog as well as a fighting dog, and had the liberty of Burke's house at 157 Albany Street in Boston.

BOUTELLE AND BURKE

To anyone who was a student of the early history of the breed, the names of John (Jack) Burke and James A. Boutelle stand out. Both Jack Meeks, in his book *Memoirs of Fighting Dogs*, and Geo. Armitage's *Thirty Years with Fighting Dogs*, mention Burke and Boutelle.

Burke was one of three brothers from Boston who lived with their sister keeping house, none ever married. He died in 1904 and we assume he was born around 1850. He fought as many dogs as anyone—prided himself on how to condition or shape a dog, and no doubt was one of the top ten dog men that Boston ever produced. Some of his dogs, the Imported Rafferty, and Burke's Tanner, a winner of several battles, were some of the good ones he owned, and they are responsible for, and back in the breeding of, the dogs in and around Boston before the turn of the century.

John Burke, at some point, teamed up with James Boutelle of Providence, RI, and they were partners for some 25 years, as their business card will attest. They had a dog called "The Gladstone" (the prefix "The" was used then: i.e., The Gashouse Dog, The Peg (a female), and The Pig, a winner in three hours and 15 minutes). Gladstone was named after William Gladstone, a political leader of England and member of Parliament for 60 years. He assisted in repealing the "Corn Laws" so that the people of Ireland would not starve. No wonder the Irish held him in such esteem!

The Gladstone had the dubious distinction of losing two money fights. In 1893 he lost to Barney Fagan's "Sport" in 57 minutes—when the referee allowed a claim of a dead dog and pronounced Sport the winner. A most unusual outcome since Gladstone later got up that same night and went back home to Providence. A little over 60 days later,

The business card of John Burke and James A. Boutelle.

Colby's Book of the

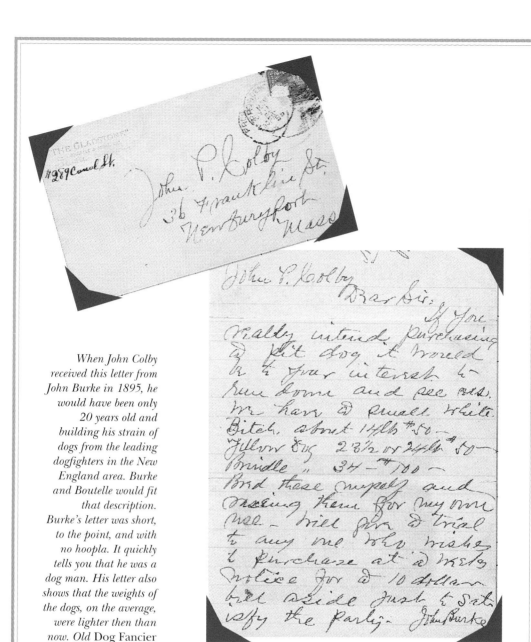

When John Colby received this letter from John Burke in 1895, he would have been only 20 years old and building his strain of dogs from the leading dogfighters in the New England area. Burke and Boutelle would fit that description. Burke's letter was short, to the point, and with no hoopla. It quickly tells you that he was a dog man. His letter also shows that the weights of the dogs, on the average, were lighter then than now. Old Dog Fancier magazine also bears this out.

Burke's letter, with the enclosed business card, was written to John Colby on November 11, 1896.

he was matched at catch-weights and lost to Jack Morrell's "Barnum." This was after being declared "dead" two months earlier.

James Boutelle was an educated man, and praised by Armitage, Meeks, and others who knew him as an honest dog man and respected for his knowledge of the fighting game. Again we can assume he was born around 1850 and when in his eighties lived in New Bedford, MA. Armitage received a letter from Bautelle in 1935 wishing him well with his book that was published the following year.

Foundation Pedigrees

Teddy Racine's Ginger

Colby's Paddy

Dick Neagle's Nell

COLBY'S TIGE (1896)

John Galvin's Pup

Colby's Jennie

Ed Donahue's Sal

Cockney Charlie Lloyd's Pilot (Imp)

Paddy Mitchell's Paddy

Cockney Charlie Lloyd's Pansy (Imp)

Jack White's Teddy

J. Sullivan's Jack

Jack Sullivan's Beck

J. Sullivan's Nell

COLBY'S PINCHER

Gallaway's Jack

Teddy Racine's Sam

T. Racine's Daisy

Colby's Pansy

Mike Lloyd's Jack

D. White's Nell

Dan Rose's Old English Rose

L. Hutton's Bill (Ireland)

J. Edward's Galtie (Imported)

L. Hutton's Kit (Ireland)

COLBY'S GALTIE (1921)

L. Hutton's Prince (Ireland)

J. Edward's Gas (Imported)

L. Hutton's Speck (Ireland)

Paddy Mitchell's Paddy

Jack White's Teddy

J. Sullivan's Beck

COLBY'S MAG

Teddy Racine's Sam

Colby's Pansy

White's Nell

Cockney Charlie Lloyd's Pilot (Imp)

Feeley's Lane Jesse

Dailey's Nettle

Con Feeley's Jesse

Lloyd's Rattler

Delihant's Peggy

Moorehead's Daisy

DELIHANT'S PADDY (1900)

Kennedy's Comsumption

Dr. Prospect's Sport

Kennedy's Kate II

Delihant's Crazy Kate (24 Pounds)

Cockney Charlie Lloyd's Pilot (IMP)

Thornton's Breeks

Unknown

Moldy McCarthy's Blind Dog

Duffy's Jack

John Duffy's Nell

Colby's Jack (aka: Lynch's Jack)

John Duffy's Jack

Kennedy's Hanna

Jim Kennedy's Blaza

COLBY'S JERRY (Circa 1900)

Jack's White Teddy

Colby's Pincher

Colby's Pansy

Colby's Peg

Colby's Tige

Colby}s Nell

Colby's Rose

1890–1910: THE GOLDEN YEARS

America at the turn of the century was a world of growth, of daring, a place where unexplored frontiers still loomed and a spirit of exploration and pride was part of the American way. The empire of the United Kingdom was still expanding its horizons with its own unique courage and pride. The dog that accompanied explorers and soldiers was still the Pit Bull, called now the American Pit Bull Terrier in America and the Staffordshire Bull Terrier in England.

Courage and honesty as well as "daring-do" were virtues held in high esteem. The worst thing that could be said about a man or boy, dog or pup, was that he was "yellow," or cowardly. Because of this, one breed found great popularity with Americans, and that breed epitomized courage and honesty—the American Pit Bull Terrier. This was the golden age of the breed; a time when the dog was appreciated, and the moral values were far different from today. If you wonder just how different the times were, consider this: President Theodore Roosevelt proudly owned an American Pit Bull Terrier while serving at the White House. A man like President Roosevelt was attracted to the honest and courageous breed. It is hard to imagine in this era of spaniels and retrievers at the White House.

Dogs were expected to take care of themselves. If it was jumped by another dog in the street, it was expected to "lick it." A dog, however, was not expected to be a bully—starting trouble in the street for no reason. Unlike today, where the vast majority of dogs are chained, kenneled, or house dogs, at the turn of the century dogs ran the streets, and only well-adjusted dogs that could find their niche in doggy society would survive. And because dogs did run the streets, they were culled for unwarranted aggression toward humans. Common sense was certainly more prevalent than now, and a dog would be excused for biting a human who was ill-treating it. But a dog that indiscriminately bit humans was sure to end up dead.

Two unidentified Colby dogs photographed at the turn of the century. Notice Franklin Street had not been paved yet.

Into this era trotted the Pit Bull at his master's heels. He definitely had a following with fighters, but he was also a darling of soldiers, firemen, loggers, and others who enjoyed his rough-and-tumble good looks and bravado. Dog shows were just becoming popular, and the new concept of breeding dogs to a physical standard of appearance rather than for useful purposes was just beginning to have a negative effect on the intelligence and soundness of the working and sporting breeds. The white Bull Terrier, strictly a show breed, was also gaining popularity. It was considered very fashionable indeed for a young gentleman to be seen about town with either a fighting cock under his arm or a Pit Bull at his heels. The more genteel of the men kept the fashionable show Bull Terrier while, as usual, the Pit Bull found more favor with the true fancier and the working man.

Fighting sports and other shows of bravado were immensely popular. Wrestling, boxing and dog and cock fighting all had their avid followers. Louis Colby explains the feeling of pride and excitement that preludes a fight: "While I was growing up, a match between a pair of dogs like Crib and Pilot fighting, it wasn't a matter of being cruel or inflicting punishment—it was similar to the feeling, though not to the same degree, as when my dad would come in and say, 'Old Jule had her pups last night,' and everybody would get excited and say 'Oh, how many, and what color, and how many males and females?' I couldn't begin to tell you how many litters we had over the years but it was the feeling of excitement and interest and that's the way it was when I was training dogs with him as a boy. If we had a match made it was a case of trying to breed something better than what the other fellow had. And faith in yourself and in your dog."

In England the Pit Bull was still unregistered, and was still known by a variety of names including Staffordshire Bulldog, Staffordshire Terrier, Pit Bull and Pit Bull Terrier. The dogs were much longer in the leg and lighter in the body than the current Staffordshire in the United Kingdom, and they were still being imported by people like J.P. Colby and bred into American lines. A man named J. Edwards, a retired bridge builder living in Nashua,

Colby's Galtie, (1912) red with a white head. He died August 23, 1921. One of the breed's great producers. This dog's parents were imported from Ireland.

Colby's Book of the

New Hampshire, was presented with a dog and a bitch, Edward's Galtie and Edward's Gas, which a financier for the New York firm he had worked for had purchased while on the trip to Ireland. A pup from a breeding of these two, also named Galtie, was purchased by Henry Colligan of Boston. Colligan was a great friend of J.P.'s, and set great store by his Galtie dog. J.P. was also impressed by the dog, and bred to him—the first outcross in the Colby strain since it was set some twenty years earlier.

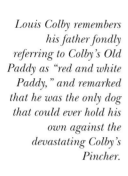

Louis Colby remembers his father fondly referring to Colby's Old Paddy as "red and white Paddy," and remarked that he was the only dog that could ever hold his own against the devastating Colby's Pincher.

J.P. bred to the dog while it was still owned by Colligan, but later he purchased Galtie. Galtie was not fought extensively though he was tested. Galtie sired a lot of good game dogs. And while he himself was quite dog-aggressive, he sired some great dogs that were not. One dog, Colby's Demo, was owned by a man living in Newburyport, who allowed Demo to run the streets at will. When J.P. wished to breed to him he would hitch Kitty up, drive through town looking for Demo, find him, bring him back and use him. Then, recalls Louis with a laugh, his father would open the barn door and push Demo out, telling him to go back to business.

Colby's Old Rose, a rugged little bitch from the turn of the century.

Many modern dog fighters tend to be impressed with "barnstormers," or dogs that are hyper and dog-aggressive, not realizing that many of the gamest dogs that ever lived were quite comfortable with other dogs.

Another famous "Major," Bowser and Tomlinson's Major, won over Ed Rubel's Shine in 2 hours and 45 minutes without a scratch (resting pause and restart of the fight). J.P. Colby bred the parents of both the contestants. This fight was reported in the *Cincinnati Enquirer*. Of this Louis Colby remarks "times have changed!" Major was a fawn dog (33 pounds) sired by a fawn dog called Spider (a.k.a.: Faust) purchased from J.P. and and out of a fawn and white bitch named Gyp. Major's breeder, H.H. Watson, stated, "Major's sire was one of the best 32-pound dogs I ever saw. There was no quit in him... he defeated the champion 32-pound dog named Cerlow, brindle and white owned by Jim Searcy. The time, 1 hour 5 minutes. This was Spider's third battle. Mr. Tomlinson got Major from one Mr. Cleaveland of Nashville." In 1906 Bowser and Tomlinson sold Major to James Evans of Salt Lake City, Utah for $500.00—a great deal of money in those days.

Bob-tail Bob (circa 1900).

Colby dogs outside the Colby house at Franklin Street. All these dogs lived at the turn of the century.

Colby's Major (1896) sire: Jack White's Teddy, dam: Colby's Pansy. This picture hangs over Louis Colby's desk to this day. Major won over Barney Fagan's Joe, of Providence, RI, in 2 hours 15 minutes at the Union House in Plainstaw, NH. On October 22, 1899. The Union House still stands.

American Pit Bull Terrier ——————————— 43

A back cover from The Dog Fancier *magazine, circa 1912. It is interesting to note the similarity between the appearance of this dog, and the early specimens of the Staffordshire Bull Terrier. Both breeds shared the same foundation dogs.*

Con Feeley's Jim pictured in Chicago around 1890. The Feeley dogs were all well respected in the Chicago area. Notice how little the breed has changed in the past 100 years. This is due to the fact that the breed has never had a wide appeal with the show ring set, and has been spared the fads of the show ring.

Colby's Book of the

Colby's Twister (1903) is not to be confused with the Colby's Twister who was the 52-pound champion of Mexico years later. Both dogs had cropped ears, similar markings and both weighed slightly over 50 pounds. This Twister weighed 54 pounds when trimmed down for fighting, and defeated Parson's Jim's Big Boy in 42 minutes at Boxford, Mass., on November 19, 1906. Twister's sire was Colby's Pincher, and his dam was Colby's Rhody.

Lemming's Butte, two-time winner over Jim French's Yellow Dog and Boyd's Malachy.

Ed Rubel of Bourbon Kennels in Louisville wrote on this photo: "Ed Rubel's Champion Dan, 42 pounds. Winner of 11 battles." Louis Colby added, "He was a white dog and sired a lot of game dogs."

Here is a copy of the original notebook kept by J.P. Colby. Note the detailed description of dogs, and the careful noting of dates. Note the reference on the top righthand corner to the breeding of a bitch named Mag to Lemming's Butte on October 24, 1906.

Colby's Mag (1896), a classic little bitch whom both J.P. and Louis called "the world's best fighting bitch ever," he was the winner of many battles, some against males. She was all white with brindle patches, and a full sister to the famous Colby's Pincher. A large framed photo of Mag hangs in the Colby dining room to this day, alongside a photo of Colby's Tige. Two greats of the Colby line. She died August 16, 1910.

Colby's Book of the

A very old article from a paper showing one of the dogs fighting for the "championship of the northwest." Joker is referred to as a "bull-terrier," a common nickname for the breed at the turn of the century

"JOKER," 26 POUND BULL TERRIER.

THE MINNEAPOLIS CANINE, NOW MATCHED TO BATTLE "WISCONSIN PADDY" FOR THE CHAMPIONSHIP OF THE NORTHWEST AND $1000.

"JOKER," 26-POUND BULL TERRIER.

[With Portrait.]

Joker, of Minnesota, 26 pound bull terrier, is matched to fight Wisconsin Paddy. He is at present owned in Stillwater, Minn. Joker is owned and handled by William Dyer, of Minneapolis, a well known dog handler. This fight is to be for $500 a side, and is to be fought under New York rules. The dogs are to check at the pit, 28 pounds. The fight is creating wide spread sensation, as it is for the championship of the Northwest, and the winner is ready to meet any dog in the world for from $500 to $1000 a side.

Some more beautiful Colby dogs from the turn of the century.

PADDY

Delihant's Paddy (1900) UKC # 69940. This fine-looking brindle and white dog was whelped May 30, 1900 and owned by W.T. Delihant of Chicago. He was the winner of five battles and the son of a bitch who also won five battles, one of which went three hours against a dog named Dooley's Duke. His grandmother, Delihant's Peggy, was the dam of J.P. Colby's Thistle.

Other pages from J.P. Colby's notebook. Here he makes reference to breeding a bitch to Duffy's Jack.

Colby's Book of the

Colby's Bill, fondly called "Yellow Bill" because of his buckskin color. Bill is in the front pen of J.P.'s kennel with one of the cockhouses in the rear. The cockhouse had 20 wall coops (5 feet wide and 4 feet high) and the fowl were tended via ladder.

John P. Colby with Colby's Bill.

Colby's Jerry (circa 1900), a very well built dog, showing a perfect tail with no curve, good angulation in the rear, nice ears and a nice overall conformation.

The home at 36 Franklin Street, Newburyport, Mass. J.P. Colby lived here for 66 years. This photo, taken about 1899, shows J.P. (left) with uncle Ben Currier. The white and spotted dog to John's left is the great Pincher. The dog in the middle between the two men is Pansy, dam of Pincher. The third dog is not identified. Louis Colby was born in this home.

In the background is the roof of J.P.'s other house, which faced Salem Street. This house was converted into a workshop, dog kennel, and stable for Kitty the standardbred horse. J.P. always meant to move his kennels out into the country, and even purchased a ballfield on the Plum Island turnpike with this in mind. The local newspaper, The Newburyport Leader, *reported that "Mr. Colby had purchased the property for the purpose of building a residence. He is a dog fancier and will probably utilize a portion of the newly acquired land for kennels. He has some prize bulldogs which are famous among dog fanciers through the country." The kennels were never built due to a combination of wet, marshy ground and severe biting-fly population. J.P. did build a barn on the property before giving up the idea, and the barn, with some alterations, stands today. Recently the Audubon Society has been negotiating to purchase some of this property and turn it into a viewpoint for bird watchers.*

Colby's Book of the

A reproduction of the "scroll" that was handwritten by John P. Colby for his son Louis while Louis was still quite young. "You might want this someday" he told Louis. Little did he know that this little work would become important as a historical document pertaining to the ancestors of just about every Pit Bull alive today.

1911–1920

"Far better it is to dare mighty things, even though checkered by failure, than to take rank with those poor spirits who neither enjoy much nor suffer much, because they live in the gray twilight that knows not victory nor defeat."
Teddy Roosevelt

To the Colby family the much-discussed term "gameness" means unyielding and determined. Louis likes the word unyielding the best, because gameness can manifest itself in many different ways. Louis describes gameness in this fashion:

"Larry Bird was on top of his game (basketball). But in his last year there was a different Larry Bird. He had a real bad back. He would lay on the hardwood floor between the times his coach would let him play. Can you imagine what it was like to lay on a hardwood floor with just a pair of shorts and a t-shirt on? But he was trying to ease his back pain. But he was determined and his love for the game just exceeded any thought of pain or personal feeling. To me, that was gameness in an athlete.

"I'll probably get shot for saying this, but three weeks ago my wife was out raking hay in the field. She was alone as the boys were off delivering hay. She went to the house for a drink of water. The old

The Colby family. Mr. and Mrs. J.P. Colby are pictured with four of their children. The last three sons had not been born when this photo was taken in 1914. John P. Jr. is standing on the rail, with Joseph L., sitting on the rail. Joseph later moved to California, where he became friends with John Fonseca, and established his own line of dogs based on his father's kennel. He wrote a small book on the breed in 1936 that is still selling well today. Marjorie is standing in front of her mother and holding a brindle pup with a white head. Daughter Helen is in J.P.'s arms. When a teenager, Helen was chosen as "Miss Massachusetts" in a beauty contest.

Colby's Book of the

dog Cleo was sleeping on the front door step and when Marie attempted to step over the dog she tripped and fell, bruising her hip and breaking her arm and wrist in two places. She was hurting so bad she couldn't get up and the only one at home was my 13-year-old grandson and he couldn't lift her, so he got down on his hands and knees beside Marie and she pulled herself up by leaning on him. So what do you think she did? Stay home or head for the hospital? No. She climbs back up into the tractor and finishes raking the field of hay so that when the boys got back they could resume the baling and get the job done. That arm hurt so much she couldn't get herself up, but she continued and finished the field simply because she was determined that that was what had to be done. That's some degree of gameness. And you would have to witness it to feel its full effect.

"We've had racing pigeons about as long as we've had dogs. A racing pigeon can race up to 1,000 miles. Four hundred to five hundred miles is rugged. If you want to put yourself in the eyes of a pigeon, you're flying home, and getting tired, maybe your wings aren't working as well as they should, it would be so easy to go down to some grain mill or church steeple, or some town hall and quit for the night—but no, it takes a good game racing pigeon to win the race.

"Gameness is such a variable thing that it is difficult to explain. You hear people talk about a dog that is a game dog, or a dead game dog, maybe

A page from the June 1912 issue of The Dog Fancier *magazine. Two ads from John P. Colby appear. Louis states, "Look at that ad, a daughter of Pincher bred to a son of Tige—what more could you want?"*

because he has won three fights or whatever. It could be one of them was 22 minutes, one in 17 minutes, maybe one in 21 minutes, but all under one half hour say, but yet, if he were to meet a more worthy opponent, there is a very good chance that he would not be as game as what was thought of him. No matter who you are, or what you are, there is always someone that is a little bit better. My brother has a racehorse, named Odin, who does very well as a trotter on New England tracks. He got invited to Saratoga to some invitational races, and that to me is the apex of racing —even the old Hollywood movies address Saratoga as such. So anyway, after winning at Saratoga, Odin got invited to Yonkers, racing against the "big boys." I sat in my livingroom and watched on TV as Odin went wire to

Another page from the June 1912 issue of The Dog Fancier.

wire, winning the race. And we were never humiliated by the big boys after that. Odin is game. He shows it in a different way. You just give Odin his head after you jockey for position, say after the first turn, you just give him a little tug on the right rein and take Odin out where he has sailing room and he just does not want another horse to go by him.

You'll see all the other drivers whipping and slashing at their horses, and with Odin all you have to do is pick up the lines, give him his head and he gives you all he's got because he is determined, or unyielding.

"No one likes a wimp. I think we all can recall having seen heroic examples of true grit, or as we call it—gameness. I've heard all sorts of ideas over the years from all sorts of dog men about just what is a game dog. My guess is, if you were to take anybody's strain, ours included, probably out of every 100 dogs there wouldn't be more than five or

ten who were completely dead game. Game cocks by nature breed more exact; if you breed a game cock and a game hen and you'll get game cocks. But if you breed a game dog and a game bitch together, you may or may not get game dogs. Some may be, but most probably won't be. The odds just work that way. By nature the game cock is the gamest of all animals. It is no wonder that South Carolina has it for its state bird.

"There is absolutely nothing you can do to an individual after it is hatched, whelped or born to make it game. Any time that a dog or chicken wants

Two pages from John P. Colby's notebook with references to several breedings to Kennedy and Lynch's Jack.

Colby's Book of the

to quit in a fight it will quit, and there is absolutely nothing you can do to change its mind. And that is why you don't want curs, or dunghills, you don't want quitters because there is absolutely nothing you can do about it. You can't make them fight. It is born in and bred in 'em."

The "born in and bred in 'em" statement applies to all areas of "gameness." You can't make a champion field dog smash into a classy point, nor can you force a game weight-pulling dog to give his best effort. The desire and love of work is bred into a dog, and into the Pit Bull has been bred an intense desire to accept any challenge, and to succeed at any task. This is what makes the sport of weight pulling such a great test for this breed: it requires strength, tenacity and drive. There is one point in favor of weight pulling as a modern test of the Pit Bull. While a dog may become a pit champion by defeating three mediocre dogs, and be himself a very mediocre dog of questionable gameness, in the sport of weight pulling the dog will always come up against an opponent (the weight) that is of unvarying quality. The weight will *always* demand that the dog give his best effort to win, for if he does not, it is very apparent for all to see.

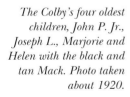

The Colby's four oldest children, John P. Jr., Joseph L., Marjorie and Helen with the black and tan Mack. Photo taken about 1920.

One dog J.P. bred that rose to fame during this time period was Harry Clark's Tramp, otherwise known as Armitage's Kager. Of this dog, Louis Colby stated the following:

"He was a great one. In the days before Prohibition a friend of J.P.'s named Nick Kelleher took a young pup to raise named Whiskey. He was named that because he followed Kelleher's whiskey wagon around Newburyport making deliveries. Like a lot of Colby dogs, Whiskey matured slowly, and he was some three years old before he got into a fight, which was in his favor for had he been dog-aggressive at a young age he would have had to have been confined. He got all kinds of exercise following the wagon around Newburyport, and that ultimately proved to his advantage. He wouldn't bother a cat or dog, minded his own business and was very controllable. But obviously after he came to fighting that closed the chapter in his life where he just followed the whiskey wagon around.

Harry Clark of Cincinnati, Ohio and Clark's Tramp (UKC 102-240) (whelped 1914). Sired by Colby's Bunch out of Colby's Goldy, bred and sold by J.P.

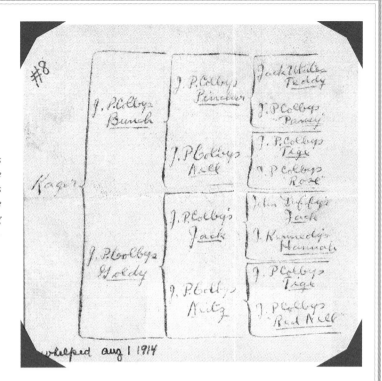

"He was first sold to a real well-known dog fighter, W.S. Semmes, and his partner Henry Jackson in Sardis, Mississippi. Sometime when he was three years old he won his first fight, defeating Joe Fromel's Teddy in Alabama on the Fourth of July, 1917. The fight lasted 23 minutes. Also in the hands of these men he stopped a dog known as Soldier's Dick at Montgomery, Alabama on October 25, 1917. This one only lasted 28 minutes. He went into the hands of a man named McLendon, and McLendon won once with him. McLendon sold him to a Dr. Harlos, and Harlos and Armitage were partners. Kager won over a dog owned by Horner and Boyle named Biter. This was at Greensburg, Pennsylvania, April 13, 1919, in 1 hour 17 minutes. He was conditioned and handled by George Armitage for this fight.

"Harry Clark was friendly with Armitage and got the dog from him. He changed the dog's name to Tramp. By now the dog had a little age on him, and when he was past the age of seven he defeated Huddle's Billy at Silver Grove, Kentucky in November, 1921. This fight lasted 31 minutes. He was conditioned and handled by Clark.

GEO. C. ARMITAGE
PLUMBING AND HEATING

BELL PHONE 677   632 STANTON AVENUE

New Kensington, Pa. April 20 1919

Mr. Jno P. Colby.

Newburyport, Mass.

Dear Sir:—

no doubt you will be surprised to hear from me. But the devil deserves his just dues. last Sunday. I fought a dog that came from you. This was the dog Rager you sold Semmes. They called him Tramp. Semmes sold him to McClendon. and he in turn shipped the dog to a Doctor here. I got him to make the match against Hoirt. & Boyle's of Johnstown Pa. for $500⁰⁰ a side at 47½ lbs. They had a dog from Dunedle a dog supposed to be a winner of 3 Battles a dog supposed to be a winner the last one he is supposed to have killed the Hoover dog in 1hr and 35 minutes at Denver, Col. He was a good fighting dog. they called him Betz it was very fast for 35 minutes Tramp was the best Betz and in a 1 shape. there dog was not over a 45 lb dog. if in shape Tramp weighed 46¾ lbs. there dog about the same. He showed he was a cur in 50 minutes. I won the fight in 1hr and 15 minutes. Now Mr Colby. you send out lots of dogs. that people say you did not and you dont send out some thing. say you do in other words if you send out a cur. They advertise you if you send out a good one they do not give you credit. In my write up. about this Battle I gave you the credit of selling this dog to Semmes it will be in may issue of the Dog Fancier. This Rager is an old looking dog. How is he Bred looks something like old cue used to own. If I had a #1.31 lb or a 38 lb one I could not

the 31 lb dog for $1000⁰⁰ against a party in Johnstown and a 38 lb one. against Horner for $300⁰⁰ Can you furnish me with such a dog. the 31 lb dog must be a fast hard Biting dog. head fighter, no legger as the dog he will go against will eat the nose off a dog that Bites his legs. I will buy either of these Weights and pay you a good price If you will ship them to me subject to approval and try out. Will put the money in any responsible mans Hands. until I have tried to my satisfaction. H. T. Clark of Cincinnati. O. Jack Wadd. of Cleveland. Ohio. or Bat Herbes of newport Ky are all good Honest men. will put money up in any one of there hands. if you doubt my Honesty. I can shape a dog as good as any man and I will bet my own money on them. The man I get the dog from gets the credit. for him. Let me hear from you If you have the Weight I want.

Yours very truly

Geo C. Armitage

P.S. I gave Redican over $1200⁰⁰ for dogs. and at last he stung me with a cur we lost $2300⁰⁰ on almost 2 years ago. But I turned around and whipped the cur that Cost us last fall with my mer dog in 37 minutes. I Handled the dog Capt. against Curry's King 2 years ago that lasted 4 hrs and 12 minutes. King was a cur but no fighting dog. Captain was game only the worse of the two

Letter to J.P. from George C. Armitage dated April 20, 1919.

Colby's Book of the

"Tramp was a 47–48-pound (pit weight) dog. He died in a kennel fight with a younger dog on Clark's place. The young dog that got loose and tackled him died two days later. Old Tramp died the same day.

"Armitage was cordial with J.P., but there was jealousy. Yet Armitage admitted J.P.'s dog was the best fighting dog he had ever seen. Tramp had a head like a water bucket—and a heart just as big."

(A letter from J.P. Colby to Mr. J.M. Jones)

My Dear Sir,   *May 11, 1917*

Yours of the 10th was just received. I would not want to sell the 34 pound dog for any less than $75.00 as I have two different parties negotiating for him that will pay $75.00 for him, and I am quite sure one of these (at the least) will send for him, as he has just won a fight with a dog I sold him.

If you want to send me a Post Office Money Order for $50.00 I will ship you the 32 pound dog I sent you a photo of, and this is an awful low price for a dog like this.

If you are not a professional dog fighter you probably think this dog is smaller than he is, he would be very thin at 32 pounds, at present he weighs 38 lbs and is not fat, I have seen him weigh 43 pounds. This dog can lick any dog living at 33 pounds, and he is big enough to fight lots of them at 34 pounds.

We fight them thinner here than they do most anywhere else. The dog I sent to St. Louis and New Orleans and Louisville to fight at 33 pounds they fought at 35 pounds, and so on.

Now this 32 pound in an absolute game dog, a great wrestler and a very hard punisher, is a nice looker, a great worker and easy to train, has nice disposition, he has a wide top skull, wide chest, tail and hair fine as silk, sound in every tooth and limb, and right in every way.

He is just as good a dog in every way as the 34 and worth just as much ("They are the best two dogs I have handled in a year"). This 32 is easy worth $100. to any man that wants a game dog or can get a match for him, or he would make you a great stud dog, as he is the best made dog you ever put your eyes on, and he has the breeding in him.

You will make a great mistake if you let this dog go by, they all have their killers and so called battle winners to sell to others, but they are seldom sold like this AT ANY PRICE as very few people have them.

With kind regards I am =
       Yours Truly,
       John. P. Colby

Webster's Joker (1914), bred by J.P. Colby and owned by W. J. Webster Jr., of Columbia, Tennessee. Sire, Colby's Bunch, dam, Colby's Rhody. Pit weight 43 pounds. This picture of Joker hung over the fireplace at 36 Franklin Street for many years.

Another dog that gained fame for J.P. as a breeder, though it did not carry his name, was Webster's Joker. Joker was bred by J.P. and whelped in 1914. Mr. Webster was the editor of the magazine called *The Pit Dog*, which was published out of Columbia, Tennessee. Joker was later sent to Harry Clark in Cinncinati, and Clark in turn let Jim Curry and Dr. Harlos have him to match. Curry and Harlos stopped a dog of Harris and Hillerich's in 20 minutes in Lexington, Kentucky in 1918. Dr. Harlos won $1,100 on this fight, quite a sum of money in those days.

J.P. Colby's Demo (UKC 189-038) a red male sired by Colby's Galtie and out of Collagan's Marshall Bitch. Demo was kept in Newburyport by John O'Donnell who ran a restaurant there on Inn Street. While bred from some of the most renowned fighting dogs in history, Demo would not bother a dog unless attacked, and ran the streets of Newburyport at will. He was a friend of a great many people around the town, especially the school children at the school yard where he visited. Demo was the sire of Colby's Brandy, a solid brindle dog with a temperament just the opposite: Brandy would grab anything that had fur and four legs, including a bitch in heat. Dog aggressiveness has no correlation to bred-in gameness.

Colby's Book of the

The front and back of Joker's stud card used by Mr. Webster.

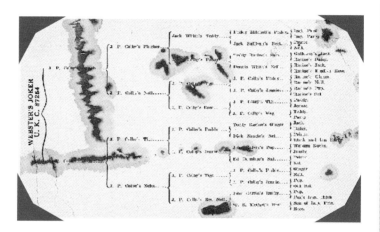

Colby's Demo.

J.P. and Louis Colby with a beautiful little bitch, "Old Gyp," in whelp. Louis recalls that his father and he were taking a break from walking the dogs when this photo was taken in 1922.

Taken at home at 36 Franklin Street, Newburyport, in 1922. The proud John P. Colby poses with Louis G. Barton and son Louis Barton Colby.

Colby's Book of the

Jim Curry's King and Geo. Armitage's Captain. This photo of both dogs with King in the foreground is a snapshot of the original picture that was over the fireplace at the 36 Franklin St. home of John P. Colby. It has now been passed on to Peter Colby, the son of Louis.
King beat Captain in 4 hours and 12 minutes on April 28, 1918 in Lexington, KY, in one of the longest fights on record.

Jack Fasig of Lancaster, PA. Jack was a heavyweight lifter and a wrestler. He was 6'5" tall and weighed 300 pounds. He is pictured here with a large Pit Bull Terrier who closely resembles the line of dogs called American Bulldogs today. This photo was taken in the early 1920s and shows that the Pit Bulldog has always come in a variety of sizes and builds.

Jack Fasig's Colby Bill, a beautiful dog that weighed 53 pounds. Jack Fasig was an admirer of both game dogs and game fowl.

American Pit Bull Terrier

DIAMOND DICK'S
"HOBO JOE"
(U. K. C. 107809)

Sixteen times pit winning son of Will's "Old Diamond Dick" and Harry Rose's "Moody Murphy." Open at stud to registered females only. Pups usually for sale sired by "Hobo Joe" and pit winning females.

Address

G. E. VOLK
Care Volk Bros. Co.
DALLAS, TEXAS

STUD FEE, $20.00

(Over)

A stud card for Diamond Dick's Hobo Joe. This dog was sired by Will's Diamond Dick, who stopped two dogs in one afternoon in 45 minutes. He also won a fight in 45 minutes in 1918 in Mexico.

John P. Colby's Bunch (1909), a brindle and white male weighing 44 pounds pit weight. This dog's name remains well known even today as an outstanding sire of fighting dogs. This photograph graced J.P.'s circular advertising treadmills and dogs for years. Bunch sired several noted dogs, including Jim Curry's Man-O-War who fought 3 hours and 50 minutes to a draw against Armitage's Bob on December 12, 1918. Probably his most famous son was Armitage's Kager. Bunch was bred to some 20 bitches in his day.

Colby's Book of the

A classic-looking Colby dog, Colby's Billy (UKC 202 762). This dog was also known as Ruschleau's Billy, and was kept for a time by Joe Ruschleau, who was J.P.'s barber and often kept dogs for him. Here Billy is nine months old and Louis is six years old.

Billy's UKC registration certificate, circa 1930.

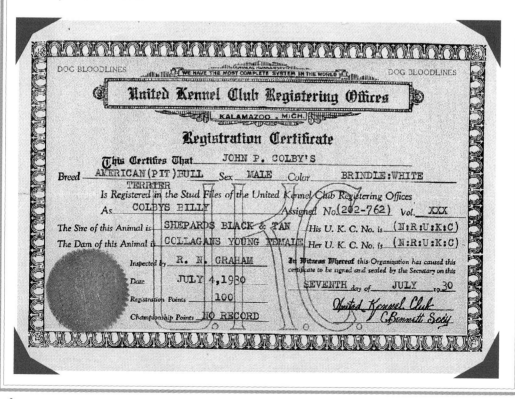

Important Pedigrees
of the 1910s

Jack White's Teddy
  Colby's Pincher
      Colby's Pansy
COLBY'S BUNCH
      Colby's Tige
  Colby's Nell
      Colby's Rose

KAGER (August 1, 1914)
      John Duffy's Jack
    Colby's Jack
      J. Kennedy's Hannah
  Colby's Goldy
      Colby's Tige
    Colby's Neitz
      Colby's Red Nell

J. Edward's Galtie (Irish Imp)
  Colby's Galtie
      J. Edward's Gass (Irish Imp)
COLBY'S DISBY
      Colby's Bunch
  Colby's Nancy
      Colby's Monkey

MESSIER'S DERRIS

Nashua Gyp

MESSIER'S OLD GYP

Colby's Black Pete

COLBY'S PINCHER

Trues' Sal

COLBY'S OLD GYP

Shepherd's Holliston Dog

WHITE'S TEDDY

Colby's Pincher

COLBY'S PANSY

H. Collagan's Mizery (sister to Bunch)

COLBY'S TIGE

Colby's Nell

COLBY'S ROSE

COLBY'S BILLY

NASHUA GYP

Colby's Black Pete

COLBY'S TRUES' SAL

Shepherd's Holliston Dog

COLBY'S PINCHER

H. Collagan's Mizery

COLBY'S NELL

H. Collagan's Young Bitch

NASHUA ZYP

Colby's Jim

COLBY'S NEITZ

Collagan's Marshall Bitch

COLBY'S BLACK PETE

Collagan's White Headed Bitch

COLBY'S COLLAGAN'S MIZERY

MEXICO

Mexico has traditionally been a land where bloodsports flourish. Bullfighting, cock fighting, and to a lesser extent, dog fighting, have all been openly practiced there. J.P. Colby, and later his son Louis, found customers and friends south of the American border. During the 1920s there was a group of well-to-do Mexican gentlemen who were

Fernando Tagle sent this photo back to J.P. with the caption written on it, "When Twister enters the ring, nobody speaks." Colby's Twister, otherwise knows as Rigolato II, was the 50–52 pound champion of Mexico. He is easily confused with the Colby's Twister whelped October 20, 1908 sired by Colby's Pincher.

not afraid to spend the money in quest of good dogs, and so J.P. sent a lot of dogs, and treadmills, and game fowl, into Mexico. During WWI and into the 1920s, dog fighting was "at an all-time high" according to Louis, in Canada, Mexico and the US. His father had quite a clientele South of the Border. Louis reflects on the difference between shipping dogs into Mexico today, as compared to the same

Twister may have been the fighting champion of Mexico, but he would still tolerate this abuse from a five-month-old male pup. Here Figaro chews the ear of the champion fighting dog with all the careless confidence of youth.

Colby's Book of the

A young Louis Colby with Colby's Bucky. A buckskin male sired by Colby's Flub Dub and out of Colby's Trixie. Bucky was raised for the Colby family by Sheriff Ayers of Newburyport. Bucky was later sold in Mexico to Miguel Gomez Reina in 1941. It is interesting to note that records show the Railway Express charges from Newburyport to Laredo were $11.41 and the health certificate was $1.00. Times sure have changed!

process in his father's day. Today, a dog can be shipped from Boston on a direct flight into Mexico, and be there in a few hours. But years ago, the dogs had to be shipped by rail, and the American trains would not go over the border. So the dogs were shipped to the railway express office in Laredo, Texas, and consigned to another Mexican agent, and then the Mexican agent would forward the dog to the new owner in Mexico. In one case, one dog broke out of its crate and killed four hogs that were being shipped before a railway agent shot and killed the dog. Another way to ship dogs was by steamer, and while they were not in the passenger business, it was a cheap way to go, and sometimes J.P. sent dogs into Mexico that way.

One of the first dogs J.P. sent into Mexico was a dog named Dixie, sold to a medical doctor named Manuel Damm in 1919. Some thirty years later, Louis had correspondence with Dr. Damm, and sent him Colby's Tweedie, which was the sire of the Dime dog.

(Letter from Dr. Manuel Damm, long-time pit dog fancier to Louis Colby.)

Dear Mr. Colby,

Glad to receive your letter and thanks a million that photo that I took over to be amplified and then I will make a picture to our livingroom; I should like and I will appreciate very much to get a photo from your good father to do the same as he was my best friend at your Country - and to him I buyed in 1919 my Dixie female that was the first Colby dog that came to Mexico City; I am in this since 1912 and I got from Albert of Ashville Ireland a couple of good pups before I got Dixie. After this one they begun to come a lot of GOOD ones from your line; Colby's Jack, Colby's Twister, - Colby's Dick - Colby's Danger - Colby's Jeff - Colby's Simon - Colby's Maga - Colby's Tunner - Colby's Leo - Colby's Bucky and some other ones; the last one was Colby's Tweedie (that is near me and sending regards to you). The COLBY name is in my heart like a miracle word that means honestly breeders and the dead game dogs. I have named to the time dogs from other breeders the "exotic strangers" as all they have NOTHING in common with that kind of dogs of the past times and with that ones from the greatest of all breeders - JOHN P. COLBY. That Gentleman that breed dogs with the principal factor - GAME, and those ones with complete ears and rat tails. That Gentleman that never speaks about color and who never has TWO TON dogs. I am really proud to say that I have the best dogs in the world but that honor is NOT MINE but for your father as my dogs are really pure Colby line. If on their pedigree you find some other names, don't worry and go back enough until you find again that miracle word - COLBY. Now I sold a lot of good ones to your country and there are a lot of real pit dogs from that dogs I sent everywhere. Mr Clarence McClain at Milwaukee, Wisc, had buyed to me Damm's (now McClain) Sylvia and Rott; the first one has a pedigree that is really a book - it is the complete story of my dogs from the first one to now; there is Galtie, Pincher, Merle, etc and by BOTH lines (sire and dam), - the Rott male dog was sired by Tweedie and whiled by my Nancy dog that is a pure Colby line for both sides. So that is really satisfactory that the old Colby's line are now at Milwaukee with an honestly right gentleman, Mr Clarence McClain. Now I sent to Mr Albert Zentz the Linda female dog. To Mr Arthur Limbeck I sent Damm's Lenny that is a well known dog for her new name Mexico's Old Glory.- Also Pain's Dillinger that is a convention winner (he won to Dees and Perdues brindle dog Oct 1952 Meridian) - Blackmore's Ruddy. - Martin's Katinka at Fort Worth. -and famous Pete Donovan Jerry that was a little brindle dog that I sent to him. I have sold also some pups and ALL THE BUYERS are PROUD of their dogs.

Of course I got the way to breed my dogs under the Mendell law and the genetic right way to do it. I have here on a chair to my favorite dog, Dora II. she is the most inbreeding dog that ever existed; Mr Martin when was here offered to me $600 and I refused as there is not money around the world to buy her. She is red, red nose 35 pound P.W. dog that is the top of all the dogs from all time. She of course IS A COLBY'S LINE.

I am jealous of what you said about fishing, horses, dogs and all that I should like to live. I am doctor in medicine and work all day long in two accidents hospital - number 4 hospital of the Seguro Social and Dep. of Federal District Hospital. I can't live like you but we never have here a hot weather; at Mexico City we have always spring times and leaves are green all the time.

My best wishes to you of the best luck from your 67 year old friend,

Manuel S. Damm, M.D.

Mexico D.F.

Colby's Book of the

(Letter from Fernando Tagle to J.P. Colby)

October 10, 1920

Dear Sir,
In reply to your favor of the 27th ultimo and trusting the dog you will send me will be the best you have, I enclose cheque No. 6282 to your order on The Equitable Trust Fund of New York for $150.00.
For your guidance I may say that Twister will fight against a magnificent dog brought over from New Orleans, this dog having won two fights killing one dog of my property that died the day following the fight from a wound in the mouth. One of the contests he won in Vera Cruz and the other one in Mexico City. The first one with $500.00 aside and the second one with $600.00 a side. The fight against my dog was for $250.00 aside and there were outside bets for up to $1000.00 I must say it is quite a sacrifice for me to spend $150 American dollars but as I am not in conformity with the death of my dog I spend it trusting that you will help me to get even in the loss of my dog for which I am so sorry. The weight of the dog is to fight Twister is 52 pounds. Could Twister do him being 2 pounds less in weight? I leave the matter in your hands and trust you will send me the best you have.
Kindly consign the dog taking care that leaves in the best of condition as regards packing, etc to Sres Benavides y Cadenas PO Box nuevo Laredo. Tam. (Mexico) to whom I will send direct orders for reshipment. Please forward me pedigree and a photo that I may identify the dog.

Yours very truly,
Fernando Tagle

(A series of letters between Arevila Hnos and J.P. Colby)

Arevila Hnos
Ave Balderas #108
Mexico, D.F.
April 20, 1922
John P Colby
Newburyport, Mass.

Dear Sir,
Having heard of the fame and fighting abilities of your dogs I take the liberty of challenging you to a fight for the Championship of Mexico.
I am the owner of a dog born here that weighs 39 pounds who is at the present time the Champion of Mexico.
Hoping to have the pleasure of an answer at your earliest convenience, I beg to remain,
Yours Truly,
Arevila

May 5, 1922

Mr Arevilla Hnos.

My Dear Sir,
In reply to your letter will say you are the challenging party so I suppose you would be willing to come half ways to fight.
Now I have a dog I will match against your dog at 39 pounds check weight in the pit for $2500 aside, if you will come to St Louis, Mo., to fight a fair Scratch in Turn fight. This is only about half way.
If these terms suit you, let me know at once and we will arrange to do business.
Hoping to hear from you, I remain,

Yours Truly,
John P Colby
36 Franklin St.,
Newburyport, Mass USA

Mexico City May 12, 1922

John P Colby
36 Franklin St
Newburyport, Mass

My Dear Sir,
In reply of your letter of the 5th we gladly accept your proposition; that's the $2500 as minimum and 39 pounds of weight but we wish that the scratch takes place here in Mexico City because the Mexican championship is going on and we want to be able to go down there and besides we want to raise among our countrymen the liking for this kind of fights, in case you are willing to come here we will invite all the American colony running at our expenses everything concerning ring, invitations and the place where the scratch is going to be.
We are not up growers of dogs we do this fights for Sport, now you can make the date for this fight and the Rules for the same we'll give you 75% of the entrance and the rest 25% for me.

Waiting for your answer your very truly,
R. Arevila

May 26, 1922

Mr Arevila Hnos,

My Dear Sir,
Your letter of the 12th was duly received, in reply will say I would not like to go all the way out there to fight as it would be quite a disadvantage to my dog after travelling so far and training in a strange climate.
I am sorry we cannot do business as other than the distance your proposition is a very fair one.

With regards, Yours Truly,
John P. Colby

One of the most famous dogs that was sent by J.P. into Mexico was A. Exchave's Jeff. A man named Octavio Larriva of Mexico City had a dog named Sordito that was considered the champion of Mexico and a challenge was issued to fight for $1000.00 a side or more. A few years before, Mr. Exchave had purchased a dog named Jack that had won a fight for him in 1920. So the following year, when Sordito was advertised as Mexican champion, Exchave wrote to J.P. looking for a dog to beat him. So he purchased the dog Jeff in 1921. The fight lasted one hour 35 minutes, and Jeff was declared the winner and new champion in Mexico. Movies were taken of this fight and shown in theaters all over Mexico. About this time, the Mexican government was trying to get the younger generation of Mexicans away from bullfighting, and so they were more lenient to dog and cock fighting. The results of fights were often seen written up in newspapers, and also shown in movie theaters.

Another man, Salvador Sanchez, bought a few dogs from J.P. He paid $160.00 for Colby's Dick, a dog that won a fight in 2 hours 40 minutes in 1922. Sanchez then sent $170.00 for two bitches, Spy and Mag, to breed to Dick.

Alberta Jauregui purchased Colby's Danger in December 1921.

Thomas Rees' "Danger" bred by John P. Colby and owned by Thomas Rees of El Oro, Mexico and Canal Zone, Panama. Circa 1915.

Colby's Book of the

1921–1945

Unlike the breeds used for guarding work, the Pit Bull Terrier was never bred to be a "one-man dog." The breed's happy, confident spirit, along with selective breeding for dogs that would transfer easily from owner to conditioner, to handler, to a new owner, and so forth, produced a stable dog comfortable with everyone around him. Other than the gun dog, few other breeds have been more carefully selected over the years to be biddable to multiple owners.

A rare and exquisite photo of Louis Colby as a 15-year-old youth. Pictured with him is his first dog, Darkey, who was given to him when he was 11 years of age. Darkey was never fought and was the perfect boyhood companion. Louis recalls her as the most intelligent, most loyal Pit Bull he has ever known. Darkey shared many important years in Louis' life, and he recalls telling her to watch over his own child when he left for the war. He states, "she meant so much to me, I felt like she was an extension of myself." This photo was taken October 4, 1936.

In the late 1980s, due to several highly publicized incidents involving careless breeders and owners, the very name of the Pit Bull became synonymous with aggression, violent behavior, and untrustworthiness. How different from the image

Colby's Dinah, a black and tan bitch who was the dam of Colby's Jule.

of the breed just a few decades before. Where once the Pit Bull had been advertised and sold as a "pal for children," (and in England as the "nursemaid dog"), now the dogs were considered highly dangerous to children, and in some cities across America, politicians, acting just as irresponsibly as the owners of the dangerous dogs responsible for human injuries and deaths, passed laws banning dogs that even looked similar to *any* of the bull-and-terrier breeds. Thousands upon thousands of kind and innocent dogs were destroyed for no other reason than their general appearance resembled that of a dog, perhaps thousands of miles away, that had caused harm.

In England, the "Dangerous Dogs Act" caused the death of thousands of innocent Pit Bulls, Staff Bulls, Bull Terriers and crossbreeds. What happened in England though, was that the very worst of the American lines had been imported, and these dogs were placed in the hands of anti-social, hostile and often criminal people, and this soon caused very negative feelings about the breed there. Very few good Pit Bulls in responsible hands have ever been seen in England, which may account for the national ban.

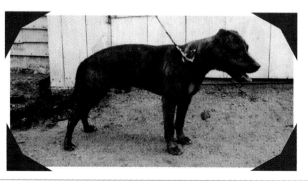

Colby's Bevoe, a brindle male. A very handsome dog. Bevoe was the sire of Ham Morris' Nervy. In Joe Colby's book that was published in 1936, Morris wrote that Nervy was "the greatest pit dog I ever owned." He said she was flawless.

Colby's Book of the

J.P. Colby Jr., and Pupsy,
a red brindle bitch
whelped in the 1930s.
She was the dam of
Colby's Buddy and
Colby's Fool. She weighed
33 pounds and was sired
by Colby's Brandy out of
Colby's Jill. Photo taken
March 10, 1940.

The sad truth is that while most Pit Bull Terriers retain their true trustworthy behavior toward children and adults, the trend toward game, calm, confident dogs has been replaced in many circles by those seeking "barnstormers" or "fight crazy" dogs. These highly aggressive, hyper dogs look game to the novice, but are more often than not displaying aggression due to some inner lack of confidence. Just as the confident man doesn't feel the need to threaten or intimidate others, the confident game dog is often the calmest and most relaxed dog. He doesn't perceive the world as a threat and sees no reason to threaten it. The temperament of the breed has been injured by those who would breed for "flash," and not "depth." The exact same deterioration of gameness is taking place in game fowl circles, where many of today's fanciers are breeding birds for the "long knife," a competition where the winner is decided within seconds, more on luck than skill. Certainly gameness has nothing to do with a ten-second cock fight. The trend, in dog fighting and in cock fighting, is to breed today for the quick, flashy fighter, instead of the game fighter.

Recently a "Pit Bull expert" with a major United States humane organization stated that the "Colby dogs are wimps, they are too calm and not aggressive enough." The ignorance behind this statement is excusable only when you consider that the majority of the dogs this man has seen have been bred by novices, punks, and newcomers, and he is unfamiliar with the true history, temperament and nature of the Pit Bull. To a novice, the Colby dogs

William H.D. Vose, of Lawrence, Massachusetts. Pictured with him is Texie. Bill Vose was an alderman in Lawrence and an avid Pit Bull Terrier fancier. A close friend of J.P. Colby for years, Bill Vose also included among his friends Jack Meeks, Harry Clark and "Red" Barber, a national radio sports broadcaster who was fondly called "the old red-head," and with whom he exchanged dogs. While Louis Colby grew up around hundreds of his father's dogs, the first dog he ever owned, Darkey, was given to him by Bill Vose.

with their inbred confidence and depth of character may appear "wimpy" as they do not feel compelled to come to pit side (or anywhere) snapping and snarling like a common cur dog. They wait, calmly, until action is needed, and then take care of business with confidence. Few old timers would be impressed with a dog that shows a "nervy" threat display.

Colby's Book of the

Earl Tudor and his Fighting Peter, the first UKC Fighting Champion.

The story of Colby's Fighting Peter is one of a dog of the old type—confident, happy and willing to work for anyone. J.P. bred Fighting Peter (Galtie x Nancy) and sold him to Francisco Cisneros of San Pedro, Mexico, on November 1, 1922. Cisneros paid $150.00 for the dog, but was unhappy when he arrived, as the dog was not as large as he had hoped for. The Mexicans tended to like large dogs, and Peter was not a large dog. He was also very good-natured, and would not bother a dog that was not facing him across a dog pit. Cisneros was disappointed with this "lack of size and fury," and felt that a fighting dog should be larger and fiercer. So Cisneros then traded Peter to Earl Tudor, who must have known that getting Peter was a real deal. Cisneros got his big dog, and Tudor got the future first UKC fighting champion of record.

When Fighting Peter arrived at Tudor's he was very thin and in poor health. Cisneros said that he had been sick for six months. Tudor wrote to J.P., letting him know that he had Peter and that he would try and do something with him.

Earl Tudor matched Peter against Dickie's Major on November 18, 1923 at Lawton, Oklahoma, and Peter won in 22 minutes. In a letter from Tom Phipps, the referee from this first fight for Peter, written to J.P., Tom had the following to say about the contest:

A rare photo showing a very young Howard Heinzl with J. P. and Bruce Johnson. Howard and Bruce, who were young men living in Chicago, were out visiting with J.P. to spend a couple weeks with him training and talking dogs. Pictured with them is the dog Sambo. Photo taken Friday, September 11, 1936.

"Earl Tudor's Fighting Peter, by your Colby's Galtie and out of Colby's Nancy. You sold this dog to a Mexican, Tudor got him from the Mexican on a trade. He weighed 33 $^1/_2$ pounds won over a 36-pound dog of our friend Dickey of Tulsa, Okla. named Major. Major was by Armitage Mike, and I don't remember the name of the bitch. This fight went 22 minutes. Peter looked like he didn't have a possible chance, was small and could not stand up with this dog, but after ten minutes, had the Dickey dog turning, Major made first scratch OK. Peter made second, good. Then on the third Major would not move out of his tracks, and I announced Tudor's Peter the winner.

"Now Colby, if a dog that I see go and take a liking to him does not either have Colby, Farmer, Noonan, Redican, Armitage, Semmes, well I soon fall out

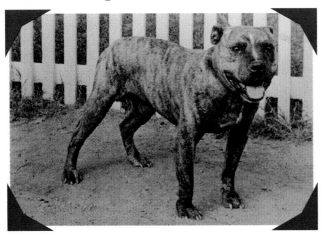

Colby's Paddy, circa 1935. One of more than a dozen dogs named "Paddy" over the last century. This dog was gray brindle and a litter brother to Colby's Rowdy. Under this photo Louis writes, "Big head, big heart."

Colby's Book of the

with him and lose confidence in him. Because we have been ruined with a few of Ginger's pups. (Ed. note: Ginger was a male dog sold to Phipps by J.P. Colby.) We bred a pure Farmer bitch, Cunningham's Dixie, to Ginger, twice, and any pup, male or female, will take their death at any time. First litter is 15 months old, second seven. I have a female left of the second, seven months old that will fight any dog she can get hold of. Have thought her dead twice, but she gets OK and soon matches her another fight. Tudor got a female out of the same litter, that money could not buy. We have lots of Ginger's pups here and they fight better and show more gameness than any of the old dogs. Everybody

There has always been a connection between the American Pit Bull Terrier and patriotism. The Pit Bull has often served as the mascot for groups of fighting men in the American and English armies from before the Civil War to today.

loves old Ginger as they have to admire that gameness. He will fight (ANYTHING) anytime, or place, and as long as he has strength enough to get back. Tudor is trying to match him at 40 pounds, would like to see him do so. Of course we can't bet an awful lot as we are not able."

Fighting Peter's second fight was also at Lawton, Oklahoma, against Langfitt's Bulger on February 3, 1924. He won this one in 22 minutes also. He then fought at Cyril, Oklahoma, on October 5, 1924, beating Davis' Ben in 53 minutes. These three fights, all "official" earned Fighting Peter the title of Champion of Record with the United Kennel Club on October 14, 1924. He was the first dog to be awarded this title by the UKC, as they had begun a championship program for dogs winning three or more "official" fights. This was quite an accomplishment for the calm, little dog that was rejected by one owner as not being large enough or fierce enough to be a good fighting dog.

There is no other breed of dog that has had so much confusion associated with its name, history and purity of type. Even admirers of the dog often are mistaken concerning the similarities and differences between the three "breeds" (American Staffordshire, Staffordshire Bull and Pit Bull) that originate directly from the original Pit Bulldog. It is

This pair of Colby dogs was purchased back from Howard Heinzl after WWII to help the Colby family reestablish their line after the interruption of the war. Pictured are Colby's Tinker (UKC 312 369) and Colby's Scarlet (UKC 288 495). These dogs enjoyed riding in the back seat of this 1940 Ford Club Coupe convertible. Says Louis Colby of this car, "I felt real swanky with that car because prior to that model you had to get out and crank down the top. This was a push-button convertible."

Colby's Book of the

often confusing, also, that because his name has never really fit, breeders and owners to this day argue about the correct name for the breed.

There will always be argument about just how much terrier blood went into the makeup of the modern Pit Bull. Assuredly there was terrier blood added, and there are strains of the dogs that are very terrier in size, character and makeup. Yet one cannot forget that the term "terrier" means a dog

The handwritten pedigree given to Louis Colby by his father in 1932. Louis recalls vividly that his father used to sit by the fire in the evenings, talking dogs with his son and reciting pedigrees from memory. This pedigree clearly shows that all the Colby dogs were direct descendants of, as J.P. Colby noted at the bottom of the page, "the best fighting dogs in England and America in the last fifty years." Louis considers this pedigree one of his most treasured possessions.

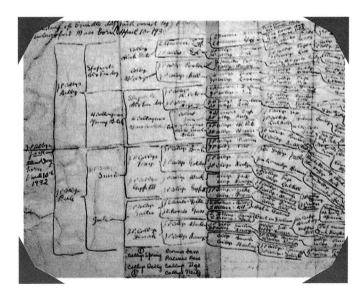

that "goes to earth" after its prey, a thing that Pit Bulls have never been developed for. Assuredly a Pit Bull *will* go to earth after prey, but it is not what he was designed and bred for. He was designed for rougher and larger prey than rats and weasels. Some fanciers cannot reconciliate with the terrier blood, others with the Bulldog blood. Either way, and considering the breed was developed in the British Isles, and not in America, the name "American Pit Bull Terrier" really leaves much to be desired.

Colby's Topsy, a flashy-looking dog with cropped ears, a fine rat tail and two black eyes! This photo taken in the 1930s outside of the kennel on Salem Street.

J. Cronin's Jack, a dog from the 1930s. Cronin used to walk dogs for J.P. when in his youth.

J.P. Colby's Fool, whelped August 11, 1937 (AKC A641507), a brindle female Pit Bull registered with the AKC as an American Staffordshire Terrier. She was a full sister to Colby's Buddy and the great granddam of Colby's Dime.

J.P. Colby obtained dogs that were bred from imported stock. These dogs came from Ireland and England, and were known as Pit Bull Terriers, and sometimes as Staffordshire Bulls after the area in England particularly noted for its pit dogs. The dogs that J.P. developed his line from were the same dogs the English developed their dogs from, which later became officially known as Staffordshire Bull Terriers. The fact that the dogs now differ in size and appearance is due not to the addition of some other breed's blood, but rather to the principles of genetics. Over time, and with the distance and isolation from each other of the two groups of dogs, the English and American dogs began to develop along slightly different lines. There are still far more similarities than differences between the two breeds.

The UKC began registering the Pit Bull in 1898, as the "American Pit Bull Terrier." The dog was never considered a show breed, and in fact the United Kennel Club only offered "Fighting Championships" to the breed. There has always been a division between working dog and show dog fanciers. Working dog owners tend to disregard show dogs, and vice versa. In the early 1930s a group of Pit Bull Terrier fanciers began to think that their breed could be better served by losing its

John Fonseca's. Tinker was a Colby dog that was sent to Fonseca from J.P. Tinker weighed 38 pounds when in condition.

Important Pedigrees
of the Period

E. MESSIER'S ZYPH

Colby's Black Pete

COLBY'S SAL

Shepard's Black & Tan Dog

COLBY'S PINCHER

H. Collagan's Mizery

COLBY'S NELL

Colby's Billy

COLBY'S BLACK PETE

Shepard's Black & Tan

H. COLLAGAN'S MIZERY

H. Collagan's Young Bitch

COLBY' JIM

H. Collagan's Marshall Bitch

COLLAGAN'S WHITE HEADED BITCH

COLBY'S DARKEY

COLBY'S GALTIE

Colby's Demo

COLLAGAN'S MARSHALL BITCH

Colby's Brandy

COLBY'S GALTIE

Colby's Jule

COLBY' DINAH

W.H. Vose's Peggy

SHEPARD'S BLACK & TAN

Colby's Billy

COLLAGAN'S YOUNG BITCH

Colby's Gyp III

COLBY'S TONY

Colby's Gyp II

COLBY'S GYP I

                              Shepard's Black & Tan Dog
                 Colby's Billy
                              Collagan's Young Bitch
Colby's Blind Jack
                              Colby's Snub
                 Colby's Belle
                              Colby's Jule
COLBY'S PADDY (1934) Gray Brindle
                              Colby's Tony
                 Colby's Snub
                              Colby's Gyp III
Colby's Maggie
                              Colby's Galtie
                 Colby's Jule
                              Colby's Dinah

                              Colby's Billy
                 Colby's Blind Jack
                              Colby's Belle
Colby's Rowdy
                              Colby's Snub
                 Colby's Maggie
                              Colby's Jule
COLBY'S FOOL
                              Colby's Demo
                 Colby's Brandy
                              Colby's Jule
Colby's Pupsy
                              Colby's Billy
                 Colby's Jill
                              Colby's Belle

"fighting dog" reputation, and taking its place as a respectable show breed. Of course there was (and still is) violent opposition to this idea by some hard-core fighting and working dog breeders. But it appears the majority of reputable breeders decided that their breed was strong enough to withstand the weakening influences of the "show ring," and that indeed, it would be nice to see the dog receive recognition for its beauty as well as its uses as a fighter, home protector, stock worker and all-around pal.

The American Kennel Club (AKC) in recent years has been one of the most vocal and confusing elements in the Pit Bull/AmStaff argument. The AKC has long tried to put forth the thought that if a certain breed is not registered with the AKC, then it is not really a breed. Tell this to the racing Greyhound, coonhunters and Alaskan sled racers, all of whom use working dogs not registered through the AKC. The truth is the AKC registered Pit Bull Terriers at the turn of the century, and the following information is in the possession of Louis B. Colby:

A Partial List of Some Pit Bull Terriers Registered by the American Kennel Club Around the Turn of the Century

Robinson's Paddy (AKC 62380) Whelped November 8, 1898, buckskin sired by Colby's Bob Tail Bob out of Colby's Pansy. Bred by J.P. Colby, owned by H.B. Robinson, Greenville, MS.

Naimour (AKC 62381) Whelped November 26, 1899, sire Colby's Bob Tail Bob out of Colby's Pansy.

Jack The Ripper II (AKC 107570) Whelped February 2, 1903, sire Colby's Tige, dam Colby's Daisy.

Colby's Tim (AKC 136015) Whelped August 10, 1905 sire Colby's Tige, dam Colby's Mag.

Plunger (AKC 107849) Whelped April 2, 1906, sire Colby's Pincher, dam Colby's Bess.

Colby's Spry (AKC 139152) Whelped December 1, 1907, a red and white male sired by Colby's Pincher out of Colby's Fanny.

Corbett's Paddy (AKC 158537) Whelped June 27, 1908, sired by Colby's Pincher out of Colby's Rhody. Louis Colby adds, "It is said that this Colby's Paddy was the winner of 12 battles. I find this hard to believe, but one of which was a win on January 1, 1912 at Fort Worth over Fisher's Skipper, who was a son of Rubel's Champion Dan. Champion Dan was a 42-pound white dog bred and owned by Ed Rubel of Bourbon Kennels in Louisville, Kentucky."

Circa 1933. Bob Tonn was the first to raise very large Pit Bull Terriers. Dogs this large have never found favor with those who work their dogs due to problems with lack of drive and wind (stamina). It is easy to see, looking at this picture, where the Pit Bulls in the background of the strain known today as "American Bulldogs" came from. States Louis Colby looking at this ad, "You're seeing too many big dogs being advertised today weighing 75–80, anywhere up to 100 pounds. They are just not the real McCoy."

STUD - - - - FEE, $100.00 CA
(Colby Bloodlines — nuf sed)

"PR" STRANGLER LEWIS (13503)
(Both quality and quantity)
World's largest Purple Ribboner, weight 103 lbs. in his stocking feet; dark brindle with splendidly white trimmings; winner of many hard fought battles and stands undefeated. We have several litters of wonderfully marked pups sired by this giant killer for sale at reasonable prices. Write to
BOB TONN (Owner)
501 Rockwood St.
Dallas, - - - Texas

***Sandoz Flo* (AKC 206995)** Whelped May 15, 1915 sired by Colby's Bunch out of Colby's Nora.

The fanciers who were ultimately responsible for gaining AKC recognition for the Pit Bull Terrier petitioned the AKC for the name "American Bull Terrier," but as there was already a "Bull Terrier" registered, which was a separate breed, the name was rejected. The fanciers were in limbo for several years, some favoring "Yankee Terrier" (as seen in the advertisements from *Dog World* magazine), others "Staffordshire Terrier." It was decided they could not use the name "Pit Bull" as they were trying to pull away from the fighting-dog image. They were hard-pressed to come up with a name that would please all, and several different names were tried out along the way. It is interesting to note that one of the main selling points of these ads was the reputation the breed had as an outstanding child's playmate and protector.

It is interesting also that the American Dog Breeders Association, which today strongly disassociates itself from AKC-registered American Staffordshires, even used the name "Staffordshire Terrier" for a while in their registry.

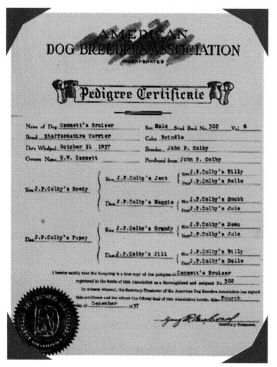

Note that this ADBA pedigree certificate lists "Cammet's Bruiser" as a Staffordshire Terrier.

Colby's Primo. Primo was triple-registered: UKC 233-460 APBT, ADBA 500-01 APBT, AKC 641-443 Staffordshire Terrier

Colby's Trim (AKC A641508) whelped June 20, 1940. A red dog with a white blaze. Sire: Colby's Pugsy, dam: Colby's Shirley.

Colby's Mabel, bred and owned by J.P. Colby. Mabel was the dam of Colby's Primo. Photo circa 1930s.

Colby's Primo, Jr. (UKC 280 001) (ADBA 500-40) whelped May 5, 1943. Primo, Jr. was bred and owned by J.P.'s son J. Richard. He was brindle with a white blaze. Sire: Colby's Primo. Dam: Colby's Merle. When bred to Colby's Peaches, Primo, Jr. produced Hennenberger's Blitzkrieg (UKC 311 546), who in turn was the sire of Hennenberger's Hunky, winner of a famous battle over Willy Lingo in Cuba.

Bob Neblett's Braddock, Jr. (UKC 50-894). A good-looking dog.

The name Staffordshire Terrier was finally decided upon, and several of the "fighting" breeders embraced the idea of AKC registration. The idea was that anything that would bring positive exposure to their dogs would be worth whatever the ultimate cost. A committee headed by W.T. Brandon was delegated to go around the nation looking at Pit Bulls and to come up with a standard based on their observations. In the yard of John P. Colby they found Colby's Primo, a dog they felt represented a sound, athletic dog. Primo was measured and observed by this committee, and the AKC standard was based in part on this dog. A picture of Primo was used to represent the standard of the

A beautiful and typey little dog (31 pounds in shape) named Colby's Brandy (UKC 207 276). Sire: Colby's Demo. Dam: Colby's Jule. While Brandy's sire, Demo, was an easygoing dog, Brandy would grab anything with four legs, and Louis writes, "Brandy was a grandson of the famous Irish import Galtie. He was a prominent stud dog during the 1930s for J.P. He would grab any dog on sight, even a bitch in heat, so we kept a very short chain for him in a corner of the workshop approximately 18 inches long, and we would back the females to him so they could not get their heads together."

Colby's Book of the

Staffordshire Terrier for many years. It is interesting indeed to compare the modern-day AKC show winners with the picture of the athletic Primo. The reader must make up his or her own mind as to how well the physical structure of the breed has fared through the years of show breeding.

The Colby family registered their dogs with the AKC as a courtesy for about three years, then returned to UKC and ADBA registry only. Many of today's American Staffordshire Terriers can look to the Colby dogs as their foundation.

J. Edward's Galtie (Imp)
   Colby's Galtie
      J. Edward's Gass (Imp)
  Colby's Demo
      Colby's Jim
   Collagan's Marshall Bitch
      Collagan's Whitehead Bitch
Colby's Brandy
      J. Edward's Galtie (Imp)
   Colby's Galtie
      J. Edward's Gass (Imp)
  Colby's Jule
      Colby's B/T Mack
   Colby's Dinah
      Colby's Nancy
COLBY'S PUPSY
      Colby's Black Pete
   Shepard's Black & Tan Dog
      Colby's Mizery
  Colby's Billy
      Shepard's Black & Tan
   Collagan's Young Bitch
      Collagan's Marshall Bitch
Colby's Jill
      Colby's Tony
   Colby's Snub
      Colby's Gyp II
  Colby's Belle
      Colby's Galtie
   Colby's Jule
      Colby's Dinah

      Shepherd's Black and Tan Dog
   Colby's Billy
      Collagan's Young Bitch
Colby's Flub Dub
      Colby's Brandy
   Colby's Chip
      Colby's Peg
CAMMETT'S FLASH (1938)
      Colby's Demo
   Colby's Brandy
      Colby's Jule
Colby's Pupsy
      Colby's Billy
   Colby's Jill
      Colby's Belle

Pedigree of Colby's Pupsy, red brindle bitch whelped June 26, 1933.

Some people are confused over the relationship between the modern-day American Staffordshire Terrier and the American Pit Bull Terrier. The letter from the Staffordshire Terrier Club of America (still in existence) to Louis Colby shows clearly that the two breeds are one. At the bottom of the page the words "formerly known as the American (Pit) Bullterrier" shows that only the name was changed when the dogs were allowed AKC registration. Since that time, the AKC has opened its stud books to the Pit Bull Terrier again, once in the early 1960s. For 50 years the two registries have bred to slightly different standards, and for different purposes. This accounts for the variations in type found within the two strains. Today with the growing interest in competing in conformation with Pit Bulls, more and more AKC dogs are being bred into UKC lines, with a resulting blurring of the differences among UKC and AKC show dogs. In the early 1990s, when specialty shows held competitions for both the AmStaff and the APBT, often AKC-registered dogs who had been dual-registered with the UKC would win the Pit Bull class. AmStaffs have been bred for over 50 years for

Cammett's Flash (whelped 1938) was shown as a Staffordshire Terrier in an AKC dog show held at the Myopia Hunt Club in Hamilton, Massachusetts, on August 26, 1939. He won Best of Breed and Best of Winners that day. Owner: C. W. Cammett. Breeder: J.P. Colby. This red and white dog is pictured here at five months of age.

uniform and correct appearance, and can usually win over performance-bred Pit Bulls at conformation shows. A person may have preference over which type of Pit Bull they prefer, the AKC type or the UKC/ADBA type, but as the letter from the STCA shows, they are all Pit Bulls.

Prior to 1960, "listed" dogs, which were UKC-registered Pit Bulls that were allowed to be shown in AKC shows but were not AKC-registrable, could be shown as AmStaffs, and there were 26 Pit Bulls who won AKC championship status as AmStaffs. Some of the more famous pit "AmStaff" champions were members of this group, such as Ch. Knight Crusader, Ch. Lylane Jill of Rossmore, Ch. Gallant

W. T. BRANDON
PRESIDENT
102 EAST HADDON AVENUE
OAKLYN, NEW JERSEY

MRS. JOHN B. McCALL
SECRETARY AND TREASURER
ROUTE NO. 2
WALLKILL, NEW YORK

STAFFORDSHIRE TERRIER CLUB
OF AMERICA
FOUNDED MAY 23, 1936

"All-American"

January 29, 1943

Mr. Louis B. Colby
36 Franklin Street
Newburyport, Mass.

Dear Mr. Colby:

Enclosed are American Kennel Club registration certificates, as follows:

#A641443   Colby's Primo, whelped May 29, 1935, sired by Colby's Brandy out of Colby's Mabel

#A641444   Colby's Buffy, whelped July 17, 1938, sired by Colby's Flub Dub out of Colby's Trixie

#A641507   Colby's Fool, whelped August 11, 1937, sired by Colby's Rowdy out of Colby's Pupsy

#A641508   Colby's Trim, whelped June 20, 1940, sired by Colby's Puggsy out of Colby's Shirley.

I notice on the A.K.C. certificate that the dam of Colby's Buffy is shown as "Colby's Trixy." Since my records show this name as "Colby's Trixie," I would appreciate your letting me know which is correct.

My files indicate that these certificates complete the applications that you had pending with the A.K.C. However, if you have others that seem to be delayed, please let me know.

Very truly yours,

W. T. Brandon

President
Staffordshire Terrier Club of America

W.T.Brandon
AA 6
Enc.4

{ *"The Grand Old Breed"*
FORMERLY KNOWN AS
THE AMERICAN (PIT) BULLTERRIER OR YANKEE TERRIER }

Letter from the Staffordshire Terrier Club of America to Colby.

STAFFORDSHIRE TERRIER

An article from the Dog World *magazine, March 1941, with a tribute to John P. Colby. This was published after his death in January of 1941.*

The 1941 specialty show is under way and will be held somewhere in Calif. A. E. Harrison, one of the vp's of the STCA and also the pres. of the Pacific Coast Staf Club, will be the head man in seeing that the '41 show goes over in a manner that will be in keeping with all the specialty shows held heretofore.

In regard to our shows, there seems to be one point that is probably over-stressed, and that is simply to build up an entry that sets a new high mark. This is all very well, but it is not primarily what we want. A large entry of poor specimens, to my way of thinking, doesn't do near so much constructive good as does a similar entry of good quality.

This brings up the old question of quantity versus quality. While we do, of course, want to build up sizeable entries at our shows, we certainly do not want to neglect the quality point. A half dozen good ones are more impressive than a dozen poor ones.—Wm. T. Brandon, 102 E. Haddon, Oaklyn, Camden, N. J.

"Fifty-two years in stafs"—that's something which cannot be said of no other person living or dead except of that grand old man who died on Jan. 24 at his home, 36 Franklin St., Newburyport, Mass.—John P. Colby. We are happy to say that his widow and son Louis B. Colby will carry on both in breeding and in marketing the well-known Colby treadmill.

John P. Colby's name takes its place among the four or five leading names in the staf fancy and no history of the breed ever will be complete without mention of him and his dogs.—W.J.

George Saddler's Duke, pit weight 39 pounds, a full brother to Emerson's Bo of Alabama. Both this photo and the one of Mike were included in a letter from George Saddler to J.P. Colby dated September 4, 1940.

George Saddler of Cleveland, Mississippi, and Mike, taken the day of the fight at 45 pounds when Mike won over Emerson's Bo in one hour 58 minutes. Saddler's Dempsey was the sire of Mike, and his dam was Colby's Misery II owned by Mr. Solomon of Cleveland.

Colby's Book of the

Ruff's Susie Q and Ch. Tacoma Cherokee Rose. Then between 1960 and 1962 the AKC opened its stud books to offspring of listed dogs, if they were bred to an AKC-registered dog or bitch. The listed dog had to have one AKC-registered dog in the first three generations and had to have a 3-point AKC show win.

J.P. Colby's dogs and his support of the AKC are important parts of American Staffordshire Terrier history.

A Pit Bull moves uptown! This handsome Pit Bull (now called a Staffordshire Terrier) is pictured at the 1939 Long Beach, California dog show. Mr. Willie Wills (of Diamond Dick fame) holds Lamb's Sir Smudgie, owned by W. Lamb of Compton, California. Sir Smudgie was sired by Lamb's Twister (UKC 230 441) bred by J.P. Colby, and his dam was Lamb's Cookie, also bred by J.P.

Ads run by the Colby family following J.P.'s death in 1941.

Colby's . . .
Noiseless Treadmills

"No Kennel Is Complete Without One"

Standard Size $25
for dogs up to 80 lbs.

Large Size $35
for dogs over 80 lbs.

ALL PRICES F. O. B.
NEWBURYPORT, MASS.

Freight Prepaid, Add $2 Extra

No Kennel Is Complete Without A Treadmill . . .

Colby's Noiseless Treadmills are for exercising all breeds of dogs. A few minutes run on the mill eliminates long walks and keeps the dog physically fit.

Matrons kept in confinement seldom produce puppies. The use of the Noiseless Treadmill will assure you of healthy offspring.

These mills are lightweight yet sturdily constructed and require small floor space. They are completely assembled and ready to operate when shipped. Any dog can run one under his own power.

* Give your dog his exercise the year round.

The back of a flyer from the Colby's offering treadmills for sale.

An ad showing a famous old dog, Brown's Tacoma Jack. This dog destroyed dogs so quickly in the pit that many questioned his gameness because he was never severely tested by another dog. The purest Tacoma Jack blood available today is present in the "Tacoma" line of American Staffordshire Terriers, of which only a very few dogs survive. Tacoma dogs were used in the foundation of the Ruffian line of AmStaffs. Tacoma Jack's pedigree goes back to Colby's Pincher twice on the sire's side.

Joseph L. Colby with John Fonseca's Rowdy. Photo taken in 1932 in Sacramento, California. Rowdy had been purchased from J.P. Colby and shipped to Fonseca in California.

Colby's Buffy. There have been two Colby's Buffys over the years. This is the original, a red and white bitch sired by Colby's Flub Dub and out of Colby's Trixie. Buffy was dual-registered with the AKC (A641444) and the ADBA (500-10) and was whelped July 17, 1938. She weighed 37 pounds. When bred to Cammett's Flash she whelped Colby's (Vose's) Merle. She was also the dam of Heinzl's Scarlet when bred to Colby's Rifle. In March of 1946, when she was eight years old, she was sent to Ham Morris of Louisville, Kentucky, one of the country's most prominent dog men at the time.

A dog Louis calls a "typical Colby dog. Brindle with even white blaze–conformation good enough for any show–and an honest disposition as well." This dog was sold to a party in Waterloo, Iowa in the 1940s.

Colby's Chinky. Louis writes, "Chinky was a beautiful black and tan colored bitch. During the period from 1945 through 1950 we had 3 other black and tans whelped–but have not had any since then. Those genes must be gone! There were a lot of good black and tan dogs in J.P.'s days, and that was one of his favorite colors. He used to remark that 'most black and tans have the finest coat'. We went many years without a buckskin, but now have three of them. We used to be able to get a black and tan by breeding a brindle to a red, but this has not produced a black and tan for several years."

Colby's Book of the

John P. Colby's Flub Dub. Photo circa 1940.

This photo from July 7, 1940, was taken at the Colby kennels at 36 Franklin Street. In the front row are (left to right) John's sons, Louis B., John P. Jr., and Alexander (Mike). Back row (left to right) J.P. Colby, Jack Johnson (former heavyweight boxing champion of the world), and Charles W. Cammett. Cammett, who was a friend of the Colby's for over 40 years, owned many good dogs, including Cammett's Rhody, Bruiser and Flash. The building to the left is the house at 19 Salem Street. This house was converted into a kennel and workshop. The lower windows are the workshop, the single higher window was Kitty's box stall. The two-story building behind Johnson and Cammett was also converted into a dog and cock house. The ground floor was gamefowl, the second floor converted into kennels.

Brindle Buffy, UKC 386-133. Sire: Colby's Mosey, Dam: Colby's Molly. The second Colby's Buffy was a brindle bitch whelped July 7, 1970, 32 years after the first Buffy. Brindle Buffy was a good brood bitch, and reared some 49 pups for Louis Colby. She is prominent in the breeding of some of the modern-day pit champions–Freddies Ch. Sinbad and also Sans Peurs Ch. Colby Pepper are two examples.

Louis Colby's Rifle (UKC 276 635). Sire: Colby's Buddy. Dam: Colby's Merle. Whelped July 31, 1942. Rifle was the grandsire of Heinzl's Peter who is back in the breeding of Mason's Hog (ADBA 22100-36).

J.P. Colby Jr., holding Colby's Buddy. Buddy was raised by the U.S. Coast Guard station on Plum Island, Mass. Buddy was later sold to Howard Heinzl and his partner Bud Borrelli of Chicago, and was fought in the Chicago area. Heinzl once wrote that Buddy was the best fighting dog he had ever seen, and ranked him number one over T-Bone and even Dibo.

Colby's Book of the

Jean Cammett romps with Cammett's Flash on Plum Island, Massachusetts. Photo taken summer of 1941.

Colby's Veronica (UKC 276 636) whelped July 31, 1942 and a litter sister to Colby's Rifle. She was named after the Hollywood actress Veronica Lake, whose trademark hairstyle had one-half her face covered in dark hair.

1946 – 1960

Louis recalls the years immediately following his father's death, "When WWII came along, my father had died several months before then, and all the Colby boys went into the service. Mike, Dick and I were all in the Army, and John was in the Navy. While we were away for 2 ¹/₂ years or longer it was very difficult. All food items were rationed, and it was difficult to feed and maintain a kennel of dogs. So my mother and my wife Marie kept the dogs going while the Colby boys were gone to war. So when I came home from the service, I wanted to start building the strain up again, and got back from Heinzl two dogs, one was Tinker and the other a red bitch named Scarlet that we had sold to him as pups. My wife and mother did keep several dogs—I don't know how, as it was very hard—and they did some breeding while we were gone."

Four Colby brothers (Joseph L. was in California at the time of this photo) circa 1946. In the rear, John P. Colby Jr., oldest son, and in the US Navy. Next to him is J. Richard Colby, the youngest son who was still in high school. J. Richard is now retired from the US Postal Service. Front left is Alexander (Mike) Colby, the second youngest son, who was in the Army. Mike built the Colby treadmills for years, and also kept a kennel. Next to him is Louis.

Of this photo Louis says: "Here's two hundred years of Pit Bull Terrier experience if you add their years with dogs together." From left to right: John Fonseca of California, Al Brown of California and later Arizona, and Howard Heinzl of Arizona.

The following is a portion of a letter sent from Earl Tudor to Pete Sparks:

Hello Pete, Well, it was good seeing you along with the other boys at the big show. I notice more talk on the breeding, lately they are talking a lot of Colby. Well I think John P. Colby bred more good ones than any man.

But just who has his old strain now? I have had them all, and will say that his dogs were the best.

Now, there is a man doing about as well as Colby. He has bred about 15 that have won the past three years, I believe he has a better record than Colby had, for the short time. That is no other than Heinzl of Arizona.

I had about run out, but he took pity on me and let me have the old Dibo dog. Now I have nothing in my yard but Dibo dogs. Have fought, or had fought 8 in past two years with 8 wins. Well Pete, here's hoping to see you at the next meet, until then take it easy,

Your Friend, Earl Tudor

Before his death Howard Heinzl wrote the following concerning the Colby dogs:

"I hope J.P. Colby's grandsons carry on with the breeding program as well as his sons did. I've had a lot of pit bulls over the years, and have 30 now. I had Dibo, both of his parents, Bouncer, and Bambi, his brother Arizona Pete, sister Lil (or Boo Boo), Tudor's White Rock, Sandy and Lucky. If I listed the top ten though, Colby's Buddy (the sire of Rifle) would have to head it. Close behind would be T Bone, (a litter brother to Colby's Dime). Gringo's dam was pure Colby (both her parents were sired by Dime). The last and maybe best dog I sent to Tudor, Lucky, was sired by Musty, a son of Peter who was also by Dime. Back when my friend Bob Hemphill still had Diamond Dick dogs, the Colby dogs were here looking just like they do now.

"J.P. put together a great family of dogs, and we all owe him our thanks, as some Colby blood flows in every Pit Bull alive today."

Louis Colby held Howard Heinzl in great esteem. He considered Howard "the number one friend and fan that the Colby family and dogs ever had." When he was a boy in Chicago, he purchased his

This photo, taken in 1947, shows Louis Colby with the two dogs he obtained back from Howard Heinzl after the end of WWII when Louis returned home and began to expand the kennel. The kennel had been kept functional by Louis's mother and his wife Marie through the war. Dogs are Colby's Scarlet (UKC 288 495), a red bitch and Colby's Tinker (UKC 312 369), a brindle and white male.

Howard Heinzl was always an admirer of the Colby strain, and built his own well-known line of dogs from dogs obtained in part from the Colby family. Here he is pictured with Heinzl's Packey, whose sire was Tudor's Bill, a son of Tudor's Dibo, and whose dam was a daughter of Dibo. The dark dog is Heinzl's Peter, whose sire was Colby's Dime, and whose dam was Colby's Tibbie. Peter was a litter brother to Bob Neblett's Congo. Louis bred this dog and gave him to his brother Dick who was in the cow business then. This little pup would sleep in the winter between the cows. One evening a cow rolled on him and broke both his front legs. The boys took popsicle sticks and fashioned splints, and soon Peter mended. Louis recalls the nomadic life of Colby's Peter, "Meanwhile my brother Mike wants to get interested in the dog game, and he wanted the Pete dog for a stud dog. So Mike and his wife Vicki get the dog and think the world of it. Jack Kelly, editor of the underground magazine Sporting Dog Journal, *was living in Long Island and he came up and saw the Peter dog and fell in love with him, and offered $400 for the dog, so Kelly bought the Peter dog, and took him back to New York with him. Then not too long after that, Kelly gives him back, because his legs were bothering him, so Mike owns Peter again. Meanwhile Frank Ferris retires from the University of Michigan, and wants to raise a few dogs in his retirement. So Ferris raised a few litters out of him. Then Ferris sends Pete on to Heinzl, and Heinzl, too, thought the world of him, and bred him. Then a friend, George Keefe drops by and mentions he is going to Alaska and wants to take a few good dogs with him to Alaska, so Heinzl lets George take him to Alaska. So up in Alaska, George was in a bar one night, and Pete was tied up outside, and somebody pulls up with a sled dog team, and Pete gets into it with a whole gang of sled dogs, and the owner of the team takes a gun and shoots him dead."*

Heinzl's Kayo. This was a pup resulting from the breeding of Tinker and Scarlet, the two dogs Louis obtained back from Heinzl after the war. Kayo was the sire of Adam's Botcher, who won a fight in 1 hour 45 minutes in Mexico. Heinzl stated that Botcher was outweighed by 4 pounds, and that he held a hold for over 30 minutes. Kayo stopped two dogs belonging to Phil Faulkner of California. Kayo stopped the "Chicago Dog" belonging to Bill Anderson in 30 minutes. A man named Richardson who was a friend of Heinzls had a large 50-pound dog named Lark. When Kayo was 8 years old he went 20 minutes against this dog in a roll, to impress some visitors. After this he was given to some friends, and lived to the age of 16. Kayo was also the sire of Heinzl's 46-pound dog Colonel, (ADBA 800-72) who was the sire of Heinzl's Tinker, a red and white dog that won four fights.

first Colby dog from J.P. paying 50 cents a week through the mail until he had paid the $12.00 purchase price on a bitch pup. He was living in Chicago, and was friends with Bruce Johnson, Bud Borelli, Rip Ryan, Joe Corvino, and the other Chicago fighters. Louis recalls of him, "In 1936, he was just a lad, I know I was 15 at the time he and Bruce and Johnson came out from Chicago and spent a couple of weeks here with us. My father was training a big brindle dog named Sambo then. Heinzl was a very, very good friend, and I cannot begin to count the number of dogs and game cocks we sent him from the time he first moved to Arizona with his two brothers Harry and Joe. He wanted to be a cowboy, and he was a good one, with his initials HWH as his brand.

"Heinzl wrote very interesting letters, and was also an envelope stuffer—he would always include a pedigree, or a humorous article, so that it was like getting a little package. It was always a pleasure to come home and find a letter from Heinzl. Heinzl bred Dibo, who was one of the better-known stud dogs in the country for several years. Another dog that Howard was famous for many years ago was Gringo. Gringo sired several good dogs, Gentle Ben, and Amos. Years before that we had sent Heinzl Colby's Brindy, later

Colby's Book of the

This photo was taken in the 1950s and shows Earl Tudor with his "sparring partners." Left to right, Dean Plemmons, Earl Tudor, Howard Heinzl, Jimmy Wimberly and Bob Hemphill.

known as Heinzl's Brindy, who was the dam of Gringo. I have a suitcase full of letters saved from Howie, and each one is a gem. I can remember he sold a dog to a young Indian boy who fought the dog for $8,000 and won. And I remember Howie saying, 'in all my years in the game I never won $8,000 fighting dogs.' Howie is far more famous for dogs he sold that won than those he used himself. The list of dogs we sent to Heinzl is lengthy. First was the female pup for $12.00. After that a dog named Sport that we sent to Howie and his

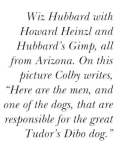

Wiz Hubbard with Howard Heinzl and Hubbard's Gimp, all from Arizona. On this picture Colby writes, "Here are the men, and one of the dogs, that are responsible for the great Tudor's Dibo dog."

partner Bruce Johnson, and also the famous brindle Buddy dog who was bred out of Rowdy and Pupsy. This Buddy dog we sent to a partner of Howie's named Bud Borelli, and Howie and Borelli won with this Buddy dog in Chicago. Howard wrote an article years later stating that of all the dogs he had seen, the number one dog had to be the Buddy dog. These dogs were all sent to him when he was a lad in Chicago. After moving to Arizona with his two brothers the list of dogs continues. We all have boo-boos. Back in 1942 my brother Joe sent us a nice red bitch named Texie from California. And she was probably the friendliest, most intelligent, best looking dog you could wish for. But Joe had never tried her out. We did not have a chance to train her and see if she was any good. About this time Howard had a match for a bitch of this size in Arizona, so we sent Texie out to him. Texie jumped the pit and Howie lost with her. So he wrote back, or phoned, and my mother said that she had someone interested in getting a Pit Bull to guard their pigeon loft. Cats are the worst enemy, after hawks, that pigeons have. So Howard sent Texie to this pigeon fancier to guard his loft. Lo and behold, about three or four years later, when he was visiting Earl Tudor, who was a close friend of his, he found the same bitch in 1946 in Tudor's yard. When Heinzl spoke of her, Tudor said that she wrecked one of his best bitches in a match and said she could fight a streak, but wouldn't scratch, just a cur, but a nice looking one.

Colby's Gus, a very beautiful white dog with brindle patches. This dog was sold to Mrs. R. S. Eiby of Jacksonville, Florida in June of 1948.

Colby's Book of the

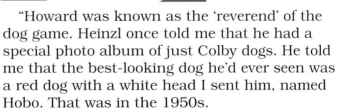

Postcard that Howard Heinzl mailed to J.P. Colby. On the back of the card reads: "My hoss's name is 'Pluto'! The black hoss with the hat is your friend Howie".

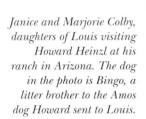

Janice and Marjorie Colby, daughters of Louis visiting Howard Heinzl at his ranch in Arizona. The dog in the photo is Bingo, a litter brother to the Amos dog Howard sent to Louis.

"Howard was known as the 'reverend' of the dog game. Heinzl once told me that he had a special photo album of just Colby dogs. He told me that the best-looking dog he'd ever seen was a red dog with a white head I sent him, named Hobo. That was in the 1950s.

"Heinzl also owned a full brother to Colby's Dime, whose name was T Bone. Originally we sold T Bone to someone else out there, and Heinzl found him in a junkyard. He was a bigger dog then Dime. We sent a brindle pup to Heinzl a few years ago and Heinzl named the pup Boom Boom because while he was holding the pup on his lap he was watching Boom Boom Mancini fight on TV. Another dog we sent to him in the recent past was a bitch named Bimbo, who was in the same litter as Colby's Galtie II, Angus, Lotus, in fact we kept that whole litter except Bimbo. She was a little easygoing dark brindle bitch."

Louis wrote to Howard Heinzl's widow after his death, telling her that "the dog game, for me, will never be the same without him."

Colby's Primo
Colby's Primo Jr
Colby's Mabel
Colby's Judo
Colby's Buddy
Colby's Veronica
Colby's Merle
COLBY'S TWEEDIE (1946)
Colby's Flub-Dub
Cammett's Flash
Colby's Pupsy
Colby's Merle
Colby's Flub-Dub
Colby's Buffy
Colby's Trixie

Colby's Tweedie (UKC 310 547) (ADBA 500-45) whelped July 25, 1946. White with brindle patches. Sire of the famous Colby's Dime. In his later years this dog was sent to Dr. Manuel Damm of Mexico City where the winter weather was easier on him.

Through Armitage's Lilly, Dibo traces directly back to Webster's Joker, Colby's Bunch, Colby's Tige and Colby's Pincher. Dibo is a name known to most serious students of the breed, for he was bred a great deal, and appears in the pedigree of a great many Pit Bull Terriers. Dibo was valued for his ability to produce fighting dogs, not necessarily for his own abilities, though he was a three-time winner. Some of Dibo's famous offspring include: White Rock, a four-time winner;

Colby's Book of the

BRUCE'S TURK

BRUCE'S JERRY

BRUCE'S LADY LOU

Corvino's Gimp

LYERLA'S MAXE

FLY OF PANAMA

ARMITAGE'S LILLY

Hubbard's Gimp

SHIPLEY'S SANDY

SHIPLEY'S RED JERRY

SHIPLEY'S MONKEY

Tudor's Goldie

TUDOR'S TURK

TUDOR'S FLASH

TUDOR'S PANSY II

Hubbard's Bounce

BRUCE'S TURK

BRUCE'S JERRY

BRUCE'S LADY LOU

Corvino's Shorty

LYERLA'S MAXE

FLY OF PANAMA

ARMITAGE'S LILLY

Hubbard's Lena

CORNWELL'S STEVE

SALABIS' MICKEY

JOHNSON CITY SALLY

Chicago Dolly

SALABIS' BATTER

SALABIS' PEGGY

LOTTIE B

TUDOR'S DIBO (1951) 47 POUNDS

DEEWEE'S SPIDER

LAURENCE'S SMOKEY

LEVERICH'S LADY LOU

Brown's Brindle Spike

WELL'S RED

LAURENCE'S HANNAH

LEE'S MOLLY

Ritcheson's Spike

DE SOTO'S KAGER

LYERLAS' BLACK SPIDER

DE SOTO'S CON FEELY

Brown's Brindle Scratch

BRUCE'S JERRY

BROWN'S CRAZY

BRUCE'S JINX

Heinzl's Bambi

CORVINO'S GIMP

HUBBARD'S GIMP

TUDOR'S GOLDIE

Ritcheson's Geep

MEEK'S BUCKY

RITCHESON'S MOUSE

MEEK'S DAISY

Ritcheson's Spotty

CORVINO'S GIMP

HUBBARD'S GIMP

TUDOR'S GOLDIE

Hubbard's Cissie

CORVINO'S SHORTY

HUBBARD'S LENA

CHICAGO DOLLY

The pedigree of Tudor's Dibo.

Tudor's Jeff, a three-time winner; Tudor's Spike, a four-time winner; Trehans Blackie, a three-time winner; Heinzl's Pauli, who went at 43 pounds; and Clancy dog, who was also a winner.

Frank Ferris was a fancier who worked for M.I.T. (Mass. Institute of Technology) during the WWII years. His specialty was making telescopes and prisms for astronomical purposes. He later did the same work for the University of Michigan. After retirement, Ferris bought a home in New Hampshire, and owned a small kennel of dogs and also kept game fowl. He purchased the American Dog Breeder's Association (ADBA) from Guy McCord of St. Paul, Minnesota. McCord was old and failing, and Ferris resurrected the ADBA and ran it from his New Hampshire address for many years. He sold the ADBA to Ralph Greenwood (who

Henry Collagan, a very close friend of J.P. Colby's for over 40 years, visiting here with Alexander (Mike) Colby. Circa 1950.

has since passed on) and Greenwood's widow and daughter continue to run it to this day. Louis Colby states the "ADBA magazine, *The APBT Gazette*, is the premier magazine for the breed today."

Henry Colligan, the lifelong friend of J.P., had a nephew who was a fireman in Quincy, Massachusetts. This nephew, Tom Colligan, became interested in the dogs after visiting with his uncle

Hubbard's Gimp (UKC 261-739) owned by Wiz Hubbard of Arizona. Gimp was a grandsire of Tudor's Dibo. Circa 1950.

Henry. Young Tom sent to Corvino's for a dog with which to challenge the Colbys. He received a bitch, and challenged the Colbys, who decided to use Connie. Tom's uncle was rather bemused with his nephew challenging his close friends. Connie defeated the Corvino bitch in about 37 minutes, and, according to Louis, "Things were different in those days—you could match a dog or fowl against a friend and win or lose everything was great afterwards. That is sometimes true today, but there is a lot of jealousy now."

Concerning his dog Dime, Louis had this to say:

"When people think of my father they think of Twister, Kager, Pincher, Joker, the Irish dog Galtie, but when people think of me, the dog that I am most noted for was called Colby's Dime. He was whelped in 1949, and I still get calls and letters from people who want pups from Dime, or who want Dime blood.

Mike Colby's Jerry II, a big "catchweight" dog (meaning over 56 pounds) sired by Colby's Rifle and out of Colby's Gypsy. Whelped 1947.

Bart and Bill Colby taken with Horner's Luger in January 1948. Luger was later sold to a man in Canada where he became the first "Staffordshire Terrier" Canadian show champion of record.

"Dime and Dibo, who was an Arizona-bred dog, were probably the two most famous sires in several decades. Their brothers, sons, and grandsons were all important to the breed. Something we never do since our strain has been going on so long is breed father to daughter, brother to sister or other extreme things you find today. However, one of the greatest litters ever born was an accidental breeding when Dime got loose and bred his own daughter, Cheyenne. There were five pups, born in February of 1958. Jack Kelly's Kayo, a three-time winner; Joe Orday's Smokey; and Jack Kelly's brindle female

Colby's Connie with Lou's oldest son, William. Circa 1950. A pretty little pup, Colby's Connie was sired by Colby's Rifle out of Colby's Bessie. When bred to Colby's Primo Jr., Connie produced Comeaux's Jolie Blond, a bitch that was sent to Louisiana and prominent in the breeding of the Cajun dogs. When bred back to her father Colby's Rifle, Connie produced Colby's Tibbie, who, when bred to Colby's Dime, produced several good game dogs. Connie's dam Bessie was sent to Earl Tudor in Oklahoma.

Colby's Book of the

Cookie was in that litter. Another litter from Dime, out of Tibbie, born in July of 1959 had Colby's Jenny, who is well known in the breeding of the Loposay dogs from North Carolina via the Chita female.

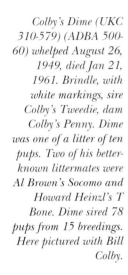

Colby's Dime (UKC 310-579) (ADBA 500-60) whelped August 26, 1949, died Jan 21, 1961. Brindle, with white markings, sire Colby's Tweedie, dam Colby's Penny. Dime was one of a litter of ten pups. Two of his better-known littermates were Al Brown's Socomo and Howard Heinzl's T Bone. Dime sired 78 pups from 15 breedings. Here pictured with Bill Colby.

"One time Pete Sparks visited here when he was living in Baltimore. He purchased a little brindle female pup named Chita. Later, when he loaded all his worldly possessions onto a flatbed truck and was moving down to Florida, he passed through North Carolina when the engine in his truck blew up. So the Loposays helped him out, and put his dogs up while his truck was being repaired, which took a few days. So in return Pete gave the Loposays the brindle Chita pup, which was pure Colby. The Loposay dogs have a great name today, and many trace back to Chita.

"The only time Dime was ever licked was by a 4-pound game hen. She had a brood of chicks with her, and one day Dime was loose and wandered too close to that hen. She took off after him and peppered his fanny all the way to the barn. You wouldn't think that of a dog who sired as many game ones as he did. He was naturally housebroken, and loved the kids. They would pick him up and carry him up to bed, and he never soiled the house."

Dime was well respected as a sire, and a partial list of some of his offspring follows:

Neblett's Little Cookie, daughter, UKC 329-547, 10/21/53, out of Colby's Margie. Cookie was the great-granddam of Maniscalco's Lady that won over Trahan's Diamond in 35 minutes at 34.5 pounds in 1960, and of Tipp's Dutch who won one in 2 hours 45 minutes at 43 pounds. She was the great-great-granddam of Al Offer's Tuffy who won over Kelly's Domino in 30 minutes at 49 pounds and over Corvino's Buddy in 3 hours 10 minutes in 1963.

Colby's Dime, whelped August 26, 1949.

Colby's Book of the

Neblett's Congo was sired by Colby's Dime.

Neblett's Congo, son, UKC 328-532, 11/16/53, 48 pounds. Bred by Mike Colby, owned by Bob Neblett of Neosho, Missouri. Congo was one of 12 pups in a litter by Colby's Dime out of Colby's Tibbie. Bob Neblett had his own strain of dogs, the most famous in fighting circles being Ch. Bucky McCoy, a five-time winner. Bob stated "every so often I get just the right Colby dog to cross into my line." Congo and a bitch called Little Cookie were examples of dogs he considered "just right." Congo was the sire of Jack Kelly's Bob Tail Buddy, who won one in 1961 at 50 pounds. He fought again, but the fight was raided and not finished. Congo also sired Cole's Pete, who won over Schumaker's Ringo in 1 hour 30 minutes in 1961. He was the grandsire of Provo's Black, who was a one-time winner; Kirkland's Sloopy, who won over Teal's Cotton in 1 hour 4 minutes in 1965 at 29 pounds; and of Tipp's Dutch, who won in 2 hours 45 minutes at 43 pounds.

Burleson or Teal's Sarge UKC 351-744, son, 10/21/53, Sarge is a grandsire to Bass Tramp's Red Boy.

Crenshaw or Hobbs' Colby Rusty UKC 329-545, son, 6/25/54, weight 36 pounds, was the sire of Crenshaw's Cahoona, who won over Creel's Sarge; Crenshaw's Goose, who won over Homer Sam's Bitch in 1961; and Crenshaw's Paddy Mack, who won over Floyd Merriman in 1 hour 17 minutes in 1959 at 40 pounds. Rusty was the grandsire of Crenshaw's Hacksaw (Freddie's Gimp) who was a five-time winner. Hacksaw won over Skagg's Keno in 35 minutes in 1966, Morfin's Perelot in 40 minutes in 1967, Thompson's Gaboon in 10 minutes in 1968, Reed's Dawg in 36 minutes in 1968 and St. Marie's Littleman in 34 minutes in 1969. Hacksaw fought at 42 pounds. Rusty was also the grandsire of Creel's Red Bitch that won over Morfin's Bitch in 25 minutes in 1961 at 44.5 pounds.

Rusty was the great grandsire of Kinard's Reno who was said to be a five-time winner, including two wins over Teal's Rock. Rusty was also the great grandsire of Sullivan's Kitty who won over Kinard's Goldie in 2 hours 15 minutes in January of 1963 at 34 pounds, and also of Elia's Patsy who won over Kinard's Dee in 41 minutes in 1963, over Coon's Bitch in 17 minutes in 1962 and again over Mayfield's Sam in one hour 32 minutes at 37 pounds. Patsy and Kitty are littermate sisters sired by Jug who was a double grandson of Rusty. Colby's Rusty appears in the pedigree of

Mike Colby with Colby's Tinker II, whelped July 10, 1959. Sire Colby's Oscar, dam Colby's Dolly. This picture was taken in May of 1963. This is a classic Colby dog, medium size, flashy markings, athletic build.

many well-known dogs such as Plumber's Ch. Alligator, Adams' and Crutchfield's Ch. Art, Lewis' Ch. Hope and Lewis' Ch. Catfish.

Colby or Spark's Texas, UKC 357-998, son, this dog, before being purchased by Pete Sparks, rode "shot gun" with the Exeter, New Hampshire animal control officer.

Heinzl's Peter UKC 331-080, son, 7/9/54, Peter is the grandsire of both Tudor's Lucky and Mason's Ch. Hog.

Colby's Dolly (Bimbo) UKC 331-079, daughter, 7/9/54, Dolly was the dam of Jim Lyman's brindle

Frank Ferris' Mac, bred by John P. Colby.

bitch that won over Kelly's White Hope in 49 minutes at 35 pounds in 1961. Dolly was also the granddam of Heinzl's Gringo. She was one of 11 pups, and her litter brother was Heinzl's Peter. Dolly was the dam of Cazzanaves' Bullet who, when seven years old, won over Kelly Bros' (Jack and Vic) Bojac at 43 pounds in 1 hour 14 minutes.

Bob Marks Milo ADBA 1200-34, son, 7/23/59, 52-pound dog kept as a housedog.

Joe Orday's Smokey UKC 352-889, son, 2/14/58. When Smokey was bred to his daughter Orday's Jet, produced Lonzo's Fay, who was the granddam of the great Ch. Homer. Homer was a four-time winner, and a game 3-hour 45-minute loser to the great Ch. Jeep. Fay was also the great-granddam of the seven-time winner Ch. Zebo.

<pre>
                        Colby's Judo
            Colby's Tweedie
                        Colby's Merle
    Colby's Dime
                        Colby's Rifle
            Colby's Penny
                        Colby's Sassy
ORDAY'S SMOKEY (1958)
                        Colby's Tweedie
            Colby's Dime
                        Colby's Penny
    Colby's Cheyenne
                        Colby's Rifle
            Colby's Tibbie
                        Colby's Connie
</pre>

Joe Orday's Smokey.

Colby's Book of the

Colby's Winnie UKC 329-548, daughter, kept as a brood bitch.

Crenshaw's Red Boy, son, 1/16/57, great grandsire of Adam's and Crutchfield's Ch. Art, and also Plumber's Alligator.

Kelly's Kayo, son, 2/14/58, a three-time winner. Kayo was first owned by Joe Blanchard. He stopped Kelly's Brandy in 24 minutes in 1959 at 46.5 pounds. He was then sold to Jack Kelly, who won two more fights with him. Kayo was out of Dime, bred back to his daughter in an accidental breeding.

Lyman's Paddy, son, 6/25/54, winner of two, the 48-pound champion of the Northeast.

Lyman's Paddy with Mike Colby.

Colby's Morgan UKC 372-731, son, 7/23/59. Morgan sired Waller's Bullger who was the grandsire of Ch. Our Gal Sunday.

Colby's Cheyenne, daughter, 1/16/57, dam of Kelly's Kayo and Orday's Smokey, both three-time winners.

Colby's Jenny UKC 372-733, daughter, 7/23/59, prominent in the Loposay strain.

Lyman's Brindle Bitch, granddaughter, won over Kelly's White Hope in 49 minutes at 35 pounds. John Shivar, referee.

Loposay's Chita UKC 368-983, granddaughter, 1/7/63, grandmother of Finley's Bo, a three-time winner. Bo was also the sire of Ch. Jeep, ROM, one of the greatest fighting dogs of all time.

Crenshaw's Hacksaw (a.k.a. Freddie's Gimp) UKC 461-979, a great-grandson who won five times.

Karen Colby (age 6) daughter of Mike Colby with a litter of pups whelped July 9, 1954. In this 11-pup litter, sired by Colby's Dime out of Colby's Tibbie, came Colby's Peter (a.k.a. Heinzl's Peter) that ended up in Alaska with George Keefe.

Louis Colby reflects on modern breeding practices, such as artificial insemination, which would make it possible for him to still be producing pups from old Dime, had the technology been available at the time when Dime lived. As a farmer, Louis's son Bruce has been using artificial insemination in his herd management for years, but is slow to accept its use in dog breeding. He states "As much as I liked Dime, who was whelped in 1945, I can see that if this genetic discovery had been available then, people could still be having pups by Dime. That's kind of hard to swallow. I think we should stick to the natural way of things."

Mike Colby with Colby's Shine, another son of Tweedie, circa 1954.

The pedigree of Henneberger's Hunky

COLBY'S DEMO
COLBY'S BRANDY
COLBY'S JULE
Colby's Primo
COLBY'S BLIND JACK
COLBY'S MABEL
COLBY'S PEGGY H
Colby's Primo Jr
COLBY'S FLUB-DUB
CAMMETT'S FLASH
COLBY'S PUPSY
Colby's Merle
COLBY'S FLUB-DUB
COLBY'S BUFFY (AKC/UKC/ADBA)
COLBY'S TRIXIE
Henneberger's Blitzkreig (brindle)
COLBY'S PADDY
COLBY'S PUGGSY
VOSE'S PEGGY
Colby's Trim
COLBY'S PRIMO
COLBY'S SHIRLEY
COLBY'S WASP
Colby's Peaches
COLBY'S BUDDY
COLBY'S RIFLE
COLBY'S MERLE
Colby's Gypsy
COLBY'S FLUB-DUB
COLBY'S BUFFY (AKC/UKC/ADBA)
COLBY'S TRIXIE

HENNEBERGER'S HUNKY AKA (SPARK'S HUNKY)

BRUCE'S TURK
BRUCE'S JERRY
BRUCE'S LADY LOU
Corvino's Shorty
LYERLA'S MAXIE
FLY OF PANAMA
ARMITAGE'S LILLY
Tudor's Joe
ARMITAGE'S BUCKO
CORVINO'S BRADDOCK
FREEPORT FANNY
Corvino's Beauty
BUTCHER BOY II
CORVINO'S BLACK PEGGY
MARKER'S PATSY
Tudor's Cherry
ALLEN'S FIGHTING TIGE
HARVEY'S RED DEVIL
TRIPLETT'S SPEEDY
Ferguson's Centipede
OWEN'S TANNER
OWEN'S MICKEY
OWEN'S RED LIL
Myer's Bonnie
HARVEY'S RED DEVIL
FERGUSON'S CENTIPEDE
OWEN'S MICKEY
Ferguson's Katie
KELLY'S WHISKEY PETE
FERGUSON'S PEGGY
KELLY'S PEGGY

Mike Colby with Colby's Tibbie, the dam of a lot of good dogs, among them Heinzl's Peter, Colby's Dolly and Bob Neblett's Congo. She was a classically pretty bitch.

Bob Neblett's Ch. Bucky McCoy (UKC 238-912), according to Louis, another "all-time great one—a big red dog with a chain weight of 67 pounds with cropped ears, a real 'looker'. He was a five-time winner and one of the gamest dogs ever bred. It is said Bucky went over two hours without a turn in sizzling heat to beat four-time winner Cranker's Black Diamond. Bucky was a great-grandson of the unbeatable Billy Sunday, an eight-time winner. Clark's Tramp (Armitage's Kager) was Bucky's great-great grandsire. Bob Neblett was active in dogs from the period roughly 1920–1960."

It has always been fashionable in the dog world to have a photo of your favorite dog on your personal Christmas cards. This one was Pete Sparks' after he retired from the government printing service and moved to Florida, purchasing a home that Joe Orday lived in. Of Pete Sparks, Louis writes, "Sparks put out the best dog magazine ever written called Your Friend And Mine. *His knowledge of dogs and printing combined to make it the best magazine that the breed has ever known. And just to update everyone, Pete lived into his nineties in Florida. His contribution via that magazine, to the dog game, will live on for generations as most of the copies have been hardcover-bound by the year of issue."*

Ed Cazzanace's Bullet, by Colby's Tweedie out of Colby's Dolly (Bimbo), white with brindle spots. A 42.5-pound dog that won a fight going over an hour when he was seven years old.

1961–1990s

"INTO THE FUTURE..."

The 1950s saw Louis Colby established as a breeder in his own right. It would be impossible for him to be compared to his father—they lived in different times and had different opportunities and challenges. J.P. Colby lived in the golden age of the American Pit Bull Terrier, when the breed was admired not only as the most capable and game fighting dog ever created by man but also as a family companion and guardian. Louis Colby lived through the most terrible decade the breed had

Taken at 15 yeard old, Heinzl's Gringo. Gringo was by Heinzl's Clancy who was a son of Tudor's Dibo. Gringo's dam was Heinzl's Brindy, who was sent to Heinzl by the Colbys. Brindy was by Lyon's Pucky and Colby's Dolly, who were both from Colby's Dime.

ever known, when the knee-jerk legislation banning or even destroying any dog that even slightly resembled a Bulldog was thought to be the answer to the problem of irresponsible owners. At the turn of the century, in J.P.'s time, things were different— there was not a constant preoccupation with lawsuits and litigation over every dog bite or fight between neighborhood dogs. Dogs were allowed to be dogs, much more than they are today. Today's dog is expected to live in much closer contact with humans and other dogs, and to understand that perhaps his "territory" is no bigger than an apartment room. Dogs can no longer wander the streets of Newburyport, or any other town. Leash laws restrict a law-abiding owner's dog's every move, and often result in neurotic or aggressive

Colby's Book of the

Colby's General Jake bred by
Louis Colby in the 1990s
and owned by grandson
Adam Colby in Texas.

American Pit Bull Terrier

Ruby, owned by John Fonseca. Ruby was out of his Colby bitch Rosa.

behavior. Yet leash laws are necessary in today's over-crowded world, and the owner that allows his Pit Bull to roam is a detriment not only to his dog but to the whole breed. Irresponsible breeding and ownership of Pit Bulldogs during the 1980s caused irreparable damage to the breed's reputation and gene pool. Pit Bulls running loose caused deaths and injuries. Pit Bulls with questionable temperaments who were not destroyed ended up biting and killing children, sometimes within the families who owned them. All these tragedies could have been avoided if fanciers had curbed their breeding practices if breeders had been more honest and professional in their selection of their breeding stock, and if breeders had not sold to irresponsible owners who could not or would not provide a proper environment for their dogs. The blame when a dog

Queenie's Rosco (P105815). Breeder Doug Jacobs, Carver, Mass. Owners: Louis B. Colby, Greg Eggleston, and Fred Bishop. Whelped 10-22-79, died February 1988. Rosco was ³/₄ Colby breeding and ¹/₄ Heinzl, having been a great-grandson of the well-known Heinzl's Gringo. Rosco sired a great many good dogs in the New England area.

Colby's Book of the

is handled irresponsibly comes first to the breeder who placed it in that situation, and then to the owner. Happily, the 1990s has seen the breed returning to a more reasonable level of popularity, and a decrease in media hype as the Rottweiler has taken the Pit Bull's place as the "fad" dog.

Louis maintained his kennel of dogs (and his game fowl) while never becoming a big breeding

A dog that is well known as a fighting dog, and producer of fighting dogs, is Garrett's Champion Jeep, ROM, who was whelped in 1976. Jeep was rather "scatter bred," meaning he was not intensely inbred as so many dogs used for fighting are, and he traces back to Colby dogs on many of his lines. Jeep was a four-time winner and won over some well-respected opponents. He won in times ranging from 28 minutes to 3 hours 45 minutes. Jeep is known more for his ability to produce champion fighting dogs, and he has earned more "Registry of Merit" points as a sire than any other dog. He produced the following pit champions: Swamp Dog, Locke's Sonny, Havanna Boy's Blondie, Miller's Cobra, Garrett's Bronco, Havanna Boy's Budweiser, Darby, Missy, Locke's Rooster, Ninja, Rebel Kennel's Turtle (ROM), Locke's Hurricane, and Tramp. He also produced three other champions, for a total of 16, as well as several one- and two-time winners. Dogs that appear in his breeding that are pure Colby dogs but do not carry the Colby name are: Loposay's Dubs, Loposay's Rusty, Burknette's Dutch, Burkette's Tiger Lilly, and Loposay's Ace. Loposay's Dot is one-half Colby breeding.

operation, and rarely advertised. He didn't need to: on the strength of his family's reputation, people still seek him out, wanting dogs and/or advice. Louis does not make his living off his dogs—he operates a working farm, and the dogs and chickens have always remained more of a labor of love than a source of income.

Fanciers new to the breed, and even old-timers who have had successes of their own, listen with respect when Louis talks about the dogs. Dog fighters, pet owners, show fanciers and working dog handlers are all interested in what Louis has to say about breeding, raising and conditioning dogs. For that reason we have printed below, in Lou's own words, his thoughts on choosing a pup and on conditioning a dog for any performance competition.

*An ad run by Louis'
brother Alexander (Mike)
in the 1960s in the
fighting dog magazine*
Your Friend and Mine.

"Before you choose the puppy, choose the breeder. Or a strain you like, or because you saw the parents and liked them. And obviously you want to get a healthy pup. So there are two things—the parentage and the health must be good. There are many, many things that people expect—but there is no way you can have a crystal ball and tell which pup is going to be the largest, most intelligent, or have the best temperament, or whether or not a dog will be show prospect. You don't have a crystal ball. I have seen people give different obstacle courses or temperament tests to the puppies. One guy in particular I know of had an intelligence test he gave every pup to see who could solve it the best. He said after a week he gave up because every time he tested them a different pup would be best. Some things of course you can tell. The basics. You can tell the sex, the color, you can tell the breeding. You can spot an obvious defect, a good tail, an even bite, a wall eye, or whatever. Those you can see.

The beautiful and classic dog bred by Louis, Colby's Galtie II (UKC 519 650) (ADBA 61000-64). This dog was very representative of the "old type," hence his name. He was 58 pounds (chain weight). Galtie II was a dog anybody would be proud to own.

"As far as character in the litter, you might find some that are more outgoing than the others, more hyper, and you'll even see some that are shy. One man's trash is another man's treasure. A doctor down in Tennessee wanted a dog that would get you dirty—meaning one that would jump all over you. I also had a man and wife from Massachusetts that were both school teachers, and they were looking at a litter that was ready to go and I said 'you may not want that one—it is more shy and withdrawn' and they said 'no, that is the one we want', because they were such a laid-back couple. So everyone isn't

Litter whelped October 1995 by Dozer out of Kellie. Who wouldn't want one of these ready-to-go Colby pups?

looking for the same thing. As a breeder I prefer that people make their own choice. Because six weeks, six months, or six years later, when the puppy doesn't turn out, I don't want people coming back and saying, 'that's not the one I wanted, I should have taken that one...' When a pup leaves here too much happens that can affect how the dog develops. Also, I like to have new owners pick up their pup at about six weeks of age. I start feeding them at three weeks on Gerber baby cereal and milk, and a little later some canned food mixed in, at five weeks I worm 'em and shortly after that I wean them. The mother doesn't do much for them after four weeks of age, other than keep them warm.

"I remember a guy who came and wanted a smaller dog, the guy was about the size of a jockey. He took the runt of the litter, named 'Dinky'. He shows up two years later and the dog was about as tall as he was! And then I sold a dog to a minister and you'd think you would try and sell a minister a dog that today would be called 'not dog-aggressive'. I recall he picked a dog that today would be called 'fight crazy', and, God, that would be the one sold to a minister!

"As far as conditioning a dog, every dog can have two weights. His best weight when in condition but still strong—that's the ultimate goal of course, to

One of the things that makes this breed attractive to so many people is the fact that they come in such a wide variety of types. This type, however, is classic, and this bitch, Colby's Lotus, along with her brother Colby's Galtie II, are some of the best-looking dogs ever bred by Louis Colby.

have your dog at the lightest weight possible but still strong, and this is either for a match or a weight pull.

"Obviously, even before you start to give your dog any work, you need to make sure the dog is in good health. I think it is a good idea to worm him. Any external parasites will make him restless, as well as any internal parasites like hookworms or whipworms, which are even more dangerous than roundworms—which look so spectacular but do far less damage to the dog. So assuming you've wormed your dog and he is in good health and free from any parasites, I think you have to take a look at him and

Colby's Bud (whelped 10/25/72, died 9/1/85).

see what kind of shape he is in before you start conditioning. A real fat dog should be put in shape to get in shape. Take that dog, and before you get him into the final 28-day keep, the dog that has been inactive and overfed, you need to get him in shape by gentle walking and control of his diet. This will help him stand the training in a couple weeks. Every dog has two weights: 1. on chain, and 2. his lightest weight, when he is light but strong, and there is always a variance of opinion on this—some might judge a dog a good 31-pound dog, and others a good 33. The only sure way to judge a dog's ideal working weight is to put him through a keep and actually condition him, or you won't know his ideal weight. There are several ways to exercise a dog. Obviously since we have made the Colby's noiseless treadmills for so many years we think there is

Colby's Dazzle (UKC G127131). Sire: Colby's Wally, dam: Colby's Peppy. Chain weight 43 pounds. Whelped 9/23/79, died 7/2/85. Louis says of Colby's Dazzle, "of all the hundreds of dogs that I have owned in my life, if I could only have one—I would just as soon have it be Dazzle. She had everything: looks, temperament, intelligence, and ability." Dazzle is the great-granddam of Sans Peurs Ch. Pepper.

nothing to compare to a treadmill to sharpen the wind and endurance in a dog. There are several other things that are good for a dog. Road work, of course, is supreme. By road work I mean taking the dog out on a leash and walking him. It's hard to get dog walkers today—everybody's busy. (Ed. note: It's also hard to find a road where you won't be plagued by uncontrolled dogs, even in so-called 'leash law' areas.). But it is the best thing for a dog to be put on a leash and walked, even before you give him any work. Some people are too lazy to walk a dog, well, ride a bike then, or even on some isolated roads, coax the dog along out the window of your car. Of course, if it's a dusty road, the dog has to breathe dust, and even on isolated roads you're apt to run into trouble with loose-running dogs. Another method of exercise is to take a long pole with a

Colby's Sue (7/15/79). Sire: Colby's Buster, dam: Colby's Nell, 46 pounds on the chain. Sue was a litter sister to Colby's Gambler (the sire of Jim Fiarris' Lilly), and she is the dam of Goodwin's Candy.

Colby's Buster (7/4/73), 52 pounds. Sire: Colby's Pete, dam: Colby's Buffy. Sire of Colby's Red. Colby's Buster a red and white dog who was a full brother to Colby's Midas, who sired a dog named Freddie's Ch. Sinbad, who, when used for fighting, won five times inside of 15 months, a feat, says Louis Colby, "not duplicated by any other dog." Buster was also a full brother to Colby's Mabel, who was the great-granddam of Sans Peur's Ch. Pepper, a six-time winner.

raccoon tail or piece of leather on the end, and the operator can stand on one spot and wave the pole around, and the dog can get lots of exercise this way. There is a train of thought on that, some people think all that lunging and braking, like when chasing a ball, could do damage to the legs, particularly the stifles. I know people who give the dogs a workout by putting muzzles on them and letting them wrestle, because no damage is done. I've no feelings one way or the other on how good that is.

"We used to have solid rubber tires, and play tug-of-war, and the dogs could not hurt their teeth. So there are several methods, but the treadmill is most efficient. In J.P.'s conditioning method you would end up with about 20 minutes mill work at the end. You start off with three or four minutes, and then on the last day have him running up to 20 minutes

Fonseca's Chris (10/10/72), owned by John Fonseca, bred by Louis Colby. Sire: Colby's Joey, dam: Colby's Mink. Pictured here at 11 years of age.

at a time. We always believed in twice-a-day workouts. There are some men promoting conditioning methods whereby you would work a dog once a day. Once a day and then they have the dog running on the mill for far beyond any time I can imagine. We like to work a dog twice a day at 12-hour intervals, like 6 a.m. and 6 p.m. Afterwards give him a rubdown and an hour later feed him. We feed the dogs twice a day, two small meals. We like to feed lean beef, sometimes raw, and sometimes boiled with the broth and a little pasta and some toast for carbohydrates. We also boil his water during a keep—I'm not a scientist, or vet, and I don't know the difference between boiled water and unboiled water. Boiled water that has been cooled down is supposed to be healthy, but don't ask me to prove it." (Editor's note: Boiled water kills germs and removes chlorine.)

Heinzl's Dunny, a red male later owned by Terry Williams in California. He was the sire of Blind Ben, who produced some good dogs in the West. He was a grandson of Heinzl's Gringo. The dam of Gringo was Heinzl's (Colby's) Brindy, who was bred by and sent to Heinzl by Alexander (Mike) Colby. She was by Lyon's Pucky, a dog that roamed the streets of Newburyport at will (much as Demo did in the earlier days). Her dam was Mike Colby's Dolly, a daughter of the famous Colby's Dime.

"To get where you want your dog to be at his best weight, it takes work and diet. That is why a dog in the hands of a good dog man stands so much better a chance than in the hands of an amateur. If you set the weight too low, and starve the dog, you weaken him. That is why you ought to put the dog through the keep before you determine his working weight.

"A treadmill is the best thing in the world—it's like a good lawyer: when you need one, nothing can be so effective or competent. But too much mill

Colby's Book of the

work without good judgment and a dog can go stale. His eyes will get glassy, his coat will get dull, and he just won't have his old zip. As J.P. said, 'A match well made is a match half won'. Don't overmatch him, and have him in good shape. Again, I can't overemphasize how good hand walking is, a couple miles a day—it just adds a bright spot to his day also. There's a lot of work to putting a dog in shape, and you can't keep him in shape year-round. Certainly here in New England with the cold winters

Colby's Red (5/12/80). This picture now graces Louis' stationery envelopes. The Colby dogs come red, but have not come red/red nose for many years.

we have, you want to feed a dog good, warm food, all he can eat, and forget about any training—just get him through the winter. We don't feel any dog should be conditioned in extreme cold weather or very hot weather. We would never think of trying to put a dog in shape under those conditions. April, May, September, and October are the months we like to condition a dog in. Common sense is a big thing. Conditioning a dog is just a case of being faithful, being honest, and using common sense.

Colby's Wally (10/1/70). Sire: Colby's Jesse, dam: Colby's Mink. A 54-pound dog who was named Wally at birth, but later earned the name of "Rocky" when he matured into a very strong and handsome dog.

COLBY'S TEXAS
(AKA: SPARKS)
Loposay's Rusty
BURKETTE'S DUTCH
Loposay's Dubs
COLBY'S BARNEY
Colby's Chita
COLBY'S JENNY
Finley's Ch. Bo (ROM)
TEAL'S JAKE
Loposay's Bullet
LOPOSAY'S BETTY
Loposay's Dot
LOPOSAY'S ACE
Burkette's Tiger Lilly
BURKETTE'S DUTCH
GARRETT'S CH. JEEP (ROM) (1976)
BOUDREAUX'S SCRUB
Boudreaux's Eli
BOUDREAUX'S CANDY
Walling's Bullyson
BOUDREAUX'S BOZE
Boudreaux's Spook
BOUDREAUX'S PENNY
Ch. Honeybunch (ROM)
TUDOR'S DIBO
Carver's Cracker
CARVER'S BLACK WIDOW
Carver's Amber
TRAHAN'S RASCAL
Trahan's Beauty T
CARVER'S BLACK WIDOW

Tudor's Dibo
Heinzl's Clancy
Heinzl's Dutchess
Heinzl's Gringo
Lyon's Pucky
Heinzl's Brindy
Colby's Dolly
COLBY'S AMOS (1970)
Heinzl's Musty
Tudor's Lucky
Little Polly
Heinzl's Margie
Heinzl's Clancy
Heinzl's Patch
Heinzl's Brindy

Colby's Prince
Colby's Jesse
Colby's Molly
Colby's Wally
Colby's Prince
Colby's Mink
Orday's Jet
COLBY'S BUD (1972)
Colby's Jesse
Colby's Mosey
Colby's Mink
Colby's Buffy
Colby's Emjay
Colby's Molly
Colby's Jill

Colby's Tinker
Colby's Russell
Colby's Bridget
Colby's Hubie
Colby's Mosey
Colby's Buffy
Colby's Molly
COLBY'S GALTIE II (8/2/78)
Colby's Prince
Colby's Jesse
Colby's Molly
Colby's Nell
Colby's Morgan
Colby's Jill
Colby's Dolly

Colby's Book of the

COLBY'S TWEEDIE
Colby's Dime
COLBY'S PENNY
Teal's Sarge
COLBY'S RIFLE
Colby's Margie
COLBY'S GYPSY
Teal's Jeff
TEAL'S JOE
Teal's Jake
SHIVAR'S BELLE
Teal's Lou
NEBLETT'S CONGO
Teal's Gyp
NEBLETT'S MITTZY McCOY

BASS' TRAMP RED BOY
COLBY'S DIME
Teal's Sarge
COLBY'S MARGIE
Teal's Jeff
TEAL'S JAKE
Teal's Lou
TEAL'S GYP
McLeod's Suzy Q Gal
STAN'S JACK
Smith's Bucky
SMITH'S DIANNE
Frank's Sugar
SMITH'S BUCKY
Risher's Ginger
RISHER'S BONNIE

COLBY'S RUSSELL
Colby's Pete
COLBY'S NELL
Colby's Buster
COLBY'S MOSEY
Colby's Buffy
COLBY'S MOLLY
Colby's Red
COLBY'S JESSE
Colby's Wally
COLBY'S MINK
Hill's Dusky
COLBY'S PETE
Colby's Peppy
COLBY'S BUFFY

COLBY'S GRIT (6/10/85)
COLBY'S RUSSELL
Colby's Hubie
COLBY'S BUFFY
Colby's Galtie II
COLBY'S JESSE
Colby's Nell
COLBY'S JILL
Colby's Uno
COLBY'S RUSSELL
Colby's Pete
COLBY'S NELL
Colby's Peppy
COLBY'S MOSEY
Colby's Buffy
COLBY'S MOLLY

Colby's Russell
Colby's Pete
Colby's Nell
Colby's Buster
Colby's Mosey
Colby's Buffy
Colby's Molly
COLBY'S RED
Colby's Jesse
Colby's Wally
Colby's Mink
Hill's Dusky
Colby's Pete
Colby's Peppy
Colby's Buffy

COLBY'S PRINCE
Colby's Jesse
COLBY'S MOLLY
Colby's Wally
COLBY'S PRINCE
Colby's Mink
ORDAY'S JET
Colby's Brendan
COLBY'S RUSSELL
Colby's Pete
COLBY'S NELL
Page's Digger
COLBY'S MOSEY
Colby's Buffy
COLBY'S MOLLY

COLBY'S DOLAN
COLBY'S TINKER II
Colby's Russell
COLBY'S BRIDGET
Colby's Hubie
COLBY'S MOSEY
Colby's Buffy
COLBY'S MOLLY
Colby's Lotus
COLBY'S PRINCE
Colby's Jesse
COLBY'S MOLLY
Colby's Nell
COLBY'S MORGAN
Colby's Jill
COLBY'S DOLLY

Colby's Beau
Smithey's Cowboy
Colby's Mabel
Fiarris' Colby's Skeeter
Colby's Gambler
Colby's Lilly
Colby's Peppy
SAN PEUR KENNEL'S CH. PEPPER
Colby's Wally
Heywood's Jocko
Colby's Mabel
Holmes' Colby Pepper
Colby's Angus
Heywood's Rasbree
Colby's Dazzle

Colby's Peggy (6/5/81). At 14 years of age she is still the Colby's house dog, and still a beautiful bitch.

Colby's Jigger (6/21/83). Sire: Heinzl's Gusto, dam: Heinzl's Loni, 33 pounds when in shape. This little dog was the last sent from Heinzl to Louis Colby before Heinzl's death.

Colby's Book of the

A pure Colby bitch, Heinzl's Bimbo and her pups by Heinzl's Willie.

Heinzl's Willie.

Two pups from Willie and Bimbo.

The rugged Colby's Buster.

Colby's Wally was bred and owned all his life (10/1/70–1/28/82) by Louis Colby, and sired several good dogs, including Colby's Brendan, Colby's Bud, Colby's Dazzle, Heywood's Jocko, and Hill's Dusky.

Colby's Tattoo (6/14/79), a brindle and white son of Colby's Lucka.

Colby's Book of the

Fonseca's Chris at 11 years of age in 1983. A pure Colby dog.

Peter L. Colby with his son Peter M. Colby stop and pose with Colby's Lotus in a shot reminiscent of the photos of J.P. with young Louis. Lotus was a littermate to Angus and Galtie II, and also Heinzl's Bimbo. Photo taken in 1982 when Lotus was heavy and in whelp to Colby's Ozark.

Peter L. Colby with his dog Angus (8/2/78) who sired a lot of good dogs.

Colby's Kelley (12/17/71). Sire: Colby's Russell, dam: Colby's Buffy. Kelley was the Colby family house dog for many years, and he placed when shown in a UKC conformation show.

Colby's Dolan (7/11/86) (died 2/22/93), a 52-pound dog that sired over 70 puppies in his lifetime.

Turner's Dime, brindle male whelped (6/1/88). Bred by Louis Colby. Sire: Colby's Dolan, dam: Colby's Uno. Photo taken at one year of age, weight 53 pounds.

A happy and affectionate bitch, Colby's Lacey, a buckskin whelped in 1989. By Dolan out of Colby's Sue.

UKC Ch. PR Pasko's Colby Sunshine (11/14/88). This beautiful bitch has been winning in the grand champion class at United Kennel Club conformation shows. She is proudly owned by Gayle Greenwood. Sire: Pasko's Colby Patches, dam: U-CD Colby's Tina. Patches is by Bud, and Tina is by Red.

Colby's Red Pepper (6/11/89), a nice red dog sired by Colby's Dolan and out of Colby's Josie. This dog is currently living in Louis' yard.

Louis Colby's brother, J. Richard and a beautiful pair of black Percherons that Louis' son Scott (at the reins) purchased in Amish country. The Colby family gives hayrides around the Newburyport area.

Christmas card featuring a favorite dog. This one is Terry William's Casey (10/14/81), a brindle male by Colby's Angus and out of Colby's Dazzle.

Henson's Sean Brutus, sired by Colby's Bud and owned by Barbara and Lenny Henson of Medford, Mass. Lenny is a District Attorney in Boston.

Colby's Book of the

Sonja Buckley, M.D., of Stamford, CT, and her dog Johnnie, who was ten years old when this photo was taken in September 1989. Dr. Buckley is a retired virologist from the Rockefeller Foundation Virus Laboratories, and later Yale University of Medicine, retiring in 1983. She and her late husband, John J. Buckley, M.D., have owned four Colby dogs over a period of 40 years. The first was a male pup from Dime and Tibbie. When they moved from a college in New York State they left the male behind as he was a friend to everyone there, roamed at free will, and "slept with every girl in the college!" Her second dog, Sheba, Sonja got from Louis in 1967, and she called Sheba her "professional" dog, as she was with Sheba when she isolated Lassa Virus, the etiologic agent of Lassa Fever. Her third dog, Johnnie, she called her "bereavement" dog, as she was great help during the illness and death of her husband. Her fourth and present dog, Tara, is her "retirement" dog.

Virginia Isaac, a national authority on canine temperament and agility training, visiting with Louis at his kennels in 1993. Virginia has long been an admirer of the Heinzl, Fonseca, and Colby dogs.

American Pit Bull Terrier

Fonseca's Cougar at 14 months of age. Louis writes of this picture, "Mr. Fonseca is 89 years old, and both he and Cougar are very active today."

Virginia Isaac of California with her Colby-bred bitch, U-CD Arizona Lady, known as Monkey. Monkey is titled in agility and obedience, and does numerous agility demonstrations on standard courses and on the much harder "Challenge Course" that Virginia invented. Monkey earned her Challenge Course title at nine months of age. As of 1994, only five dogs had earned this title.

Colby's Book of the

Dr. Sonja Buckley's "retirement" dog, Tara Colby, whelped 4/13/91. She is the most intelligent and aggressive of the three females. Being alone, Dr. Buckley says, "without Tara I would have to sell my home, but with her I feel safe, and we have a very nice life together."

Photo of two male Pit Bulls doing obedience as a team, using one leash to couple them together. On left is Spartan's Samson, U-CD, CD, U-CDX, TT, CGC, AG I, AG II–a one-half Colby dog. On the right is Fonseca's H.K. Spot, TT, a Colby dog. Both owned and trained by Virginia Isaac.

Ian Phipps of Tallahassee, FL, with his dog Spunk windsurfing. Spunk was born in 1989, sired by Dolan and out of Colby's Cookie.

Colby's Chester (11/4/85) sired by Colby's Angus. Dam: Colby's Freda. Here Chester is posing with his new harness.

Virginia Isaac's Fonseca's H.K. Arizona Lady, U-CD, CGC, AG I, AGII, ATCH, called Monkey, a Colby dog, negotiating the advanced agility obstacle called the "wicked wicket walk." Its purpose is to teach the dog to use each foot independently. Monkey was the first Pit Bull to earn the Agility Trial Championship.

A scene from the 1992 national ADBA convention, where Louis Colby was a guest of honor. Pictured are (left to right): Louis Colby; David and Coleen Hill, pulling enthusiasts from Texas; Gary Hammonds, a conformation judge from Texas; and Ed Hinkle of Texas, a host of the show.

A Colby's noiseless treadmill was the grand prize at the 1992 ADBA national convention raffle.

Louis Colby was very proud and pleased to see this picture offered as a prize at the national, a picture of the head of Colby's Galtie II imposed on the Texas state flag and framed in gold. This was one of the prizes at the "Endangered Breed Association" booth at the 1992 ADBA nationals.

Louis Colby holding his great-granddaughter Sarah Elizabeth Colby, while granddaughter Rachel Colby and daughter-in-law Cindy Colby look on.

Colby's Ginger, a red female whelped 8/18/91. Sire: Colby's Grit, dam: Colby's Lacey. This close-up of Ginger's head illustrates some of the fine points that judges in conformation shows should be aware of: An absence of heavy jowls (lippiness), fine hair and smooth to the touch, small natural thin ears that drop before the eyes, broad and slightly rounded skull and, of course, an even bite.

Colby's Ivy (1990), currently living in Louis' yard.

Spunk, a Colby dog, rides behind his master's bike in comfort.

Spunk, owned by the Phipps family of Florida, with the other Phipps dogs.

Colby's Thistle II, a red female whelped 7/11/86. Sire: Colby's Brendan, dam: Colby's Lotus. This shot was taken right after a snowstorm in the winter of 1993. The cockpens to the right are empty, as the cocks stay inside the barn and out of the cold during the cold Massachusetts winters.

The day after a 1993 snowstorm. Colby's Bonnie stands in front, Colby's Ginger is at the far left, Colby's Red Pepper is behind Bonnie, and Colby's Zorro is in the rear to the right. Only a snug, dry dog house full of bedding will allow a shorthaired breed like the Pit Bull to survive outside.

The doghouses made and used by the Colby family for years. Insulated, in winter they sport a sturdy flap to conserve body heat. Metal flashing around the edges keeps some dogs from chewing on the door and destroying the structure.

The Colby kennels and cockhouse in winter. New England gets large amounts of snow and bitter cold weather.

Part of the Colby kennels taken in the winter of 1993. Colby's Milo is in the front right, and Colby's Ivy is to Milo's right.

Colby's Grit (6/10/85) shown here in the summer of 1993 at eight years of age. Sire: Colby's Red, dam: Colby's Uno. Grit may have sired more Colby pups than any previous Colby dog. Since 1987, Grit has sired 146 pups. He has been bred to about 20 bitches, including Colby's Thistle, who produced 34 pups from Grit in four litters.

Patch at 3 ¹/₂ months of age trying to take a stick away from his pal Thumper. "Just a few more months, Patch, and it should get easier..." Owned by Linda Pesaturo, Danbury, N.H.

Colby's Big Guy, currently living with Louis. Of this dog Louis states, "He has all the qualifications that you would need for anything. Perfect-shaped skull, ears far apart, perfect rose ears, drop before eyes, even white blaze, stands well and typical of the breed. You could find him in anybody's yard, anywhere in the United States, and know he was a Colby dog."

Colby's Grit, sire of 146 pups. A handsome and worthy dog.

Colby's Book of the

J. Richard Colby, youngest son of J.P., giving hay rides with Willie and Bob, blonde Belgians. This impressive team weighs in at 4400 pounds.

Colby's Dee Dee, whelped 9/30/92. Sire: Colby's Grit, dam: Colby's Bonnie. This photo was taken just prior to her whelping her first litter. She is a granddaughter of Heywood's Rasbree.

Linda Pesaturo's Patch, whelped 8/18/91. Sire: Colby's Grit, dam: Colby's Lacey.

American Pit Bull Terrier

Colby's Lucy (9/30/92), bred by Louis Colby, owned by John R. Colby of Duncanville, Texas. Lucy, as is San Peur's Ch. Pepper, is granddaughter of the famous Heywood's Rasbree (a pure Colby bitch).

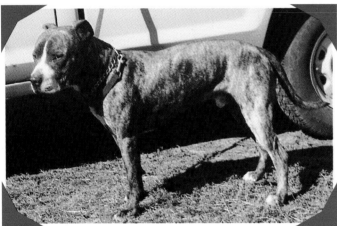

"The Hydrant Dog," thus named because Louis found the dog tied to a hydrant outside his Newburyport home when the owner was apparently no longer able to care for him. "Unlike most kennel dogs," says Louis, "he was housebroken, liked to ride in the car, was trained to do tricks, was a good watchdog and a perfect specimen of the breed."

Barbara Brzezinski, sister-in-law of Peter Colby, with Colby's Bud II, an old-timer in this photo, and a near-perfect replica of the original Colby's Bud.

Peter Colby's Otis, sired by Colby's Bud II out of Colby's Kirby.

Colby's Book of the

Colby's Zorro (UKC G606223) (ADBA 46500E-00) whelped 9/27/90 by Colby's Grit ex Colby's Thistle. Louis says, "Zorro is one of the premier stud dogs in our kennel today. He is the color of gold–with a big heart that matches his color."

Colby's Willie (1992). Sire: Colby's Grit, dam: Colby's Ivy. Willie is slightly larger than the average Colby-bred dog, as he will mature over the standard weight of 65 pounds.

Colby's Milo (5/9/90).
Sire: Colby's Dolan, dam:
Heywood's Rasbree.

Colby's Dozer, bred and
owned by Peter Colby.

Peter Colby with Colby's Bodger, sired by Colby's Bud II and out of Colby's Lacey. Photo taken May 1994, just prior to Bodger being exported to Pakistan.

Louis Colby and John Fonseca of California. Photo taken in the Colby kennel yard when John came for a visit in 1988. John has been involved in the breed since his youth. He knew most of the people involved in the breed west of the Mississippi.

Rodger Scott of Tulsa, OK, with Scott's Neblett Blondie. Rodger is a fan of the Neblett bloodline, and one of the most popular judges for the ADBA. Louis states, "Rodger visited our kennel in 1992. The breed is lucky to have men like Rodger in its corner."

An endearing photo of two cute youngsters. Sarah Elizabeth Colby of Red Oak, Texas, is the fifth generation of the Colby family to be involved with the breed. J.P. was her great-great grandfather, and his dogs were the ancestors of her pup Colby's Jake, whelped Christmas Day, 1993.

O'Donovan's Blue Rage (2/7/93), shown here taking second place in the female puppy class at the 1993 UKC national. Rage is owned by Holly Strychalski of Lynn, Massachusetts.

Colby's Book of the

*"Into the future we go..."
Despite media hype and
irresponsible legislation,
the American Pit Bull
Terrier is still the grand
old breed, and still the
best pal a kid can have.
Sturdy and patient, they
tolerate children unlike
more nervous or
defensive breeds can.
Here Silva's Victory (a
Colby bitch), owned by
Daniel Silva pulls
Brandi L. Silva in the
Memorial Day parade in
Littleton, NH. To their
owners, no other breed
can hold the same in the
heart that a good Pit
Bull can. Their strength,
courage, grit, and even
nature set an example we
should all live by. They
are true heroes, often
misunderstood in a
modern world that has
moved so far away from
the virtues that made
survival possible in the
harsh and challenging
past. They are indeed a
direct link to the past,
with the strength and
skill necessary to survive
and assist man in the
harshest environments
and doing the roughest
sort of work, yet they are
adaptable enough to be
able to live "uptown,"
and take over "child
sitting" duties if need be.
No other breed has the
potential to be so many
things, and the
determination to
complete whatever task is
asked of it.*

American Pit Bull Terrier

FINAL THOUGHTS

The history of most purebred dogs, as recognizable breeds, goes back only a hundred years or so. A few utilitarian dog types stretch back into our shared history a thousand years or more. One such type of dog is the gripping/fighting dog, whose ancestors were tough hunting dogs bred to close in and grasp the hunter's prey. These dogs were also developed into gladiators to entertain blood-sport enthusiasts.

Colby's Sue (7/15/79) and a littermate as pups bred from Colby's Buster and Nell.

This type of dog has been known by many names in many ages: Alaunt, Bullenbeisser, Bulldog, Pit Bulldog, Pit Terrier, Staffordshire—a name to please every group of fanciers. Today he is best represented by the much maligned and little understood breed most often called "Pit Bull." The Pit Bull can trace its roots back in time as far, in many cases farther, than most breeds. His kind have been bred since the dawn of man as a hunter, fighter, and controller of stock. He has been valued for his grit, guts, "bulldog" determination and intelligence. Like it or not, it was those jobs, and the natural selection associated with those jobs that produced the brave, loyal, daring and amiable dog we have today. One does not have to approve of blood sports to at least acknowledge what part they played in the development of game animals. For John and Louis Colby, and people like them, the matching of dogs seems natural and pleasant. They do it for entertainment, they do it for money, and they do it for the love of the game dog. It is not the intent of this book to condone or condemn the fighting of dogs—that is a personal and political issue. It is the story of one family's stewardship of the breed, and the resulting line of dogs that have become famous in the world over, and who feature in the pedigree of just about every American Pit Bull Terrier alive today. That stewardship stretches from before the turn of the century, when dogs were still being imported from the United Kingdom on a regular basis, to today, when the son of J.P. Colby continues to breed the line as we enter another century. In one hundred years the dogs have changed very little, as is the way with any working breed. Show fads may ruin certain lines of show-bred Pit Bulls, but for the Colby line, time and fads have not changed the basics of the breed.

Colby's Lucka (UKC 817 115A), red and white male whelped 10-25-72, died 5-27-82. Sire: Colby's Wally, dam: Colby's Buffy. Says Louis of Lucka: "A few years ago my daughter Marjorie obtained a job teaching school in Malden, Mass. and was living alone. One weekend she came home and said she needed a dog for a companion and guardian. A puppy, of course, would not fill the bill as a guardian, so I told her to take Lucka. Marjorie gained much respect from the students after that, as they would say, 'Miss Colby has a Pit Bull,' when viewing her walking Lucka before and after school hours."

Colby's Peggy (whelped 06/05/81), 13 years old in this picture. Peggy was the Colby's house dog for many years. Louis particularly likes Peggy's head type.

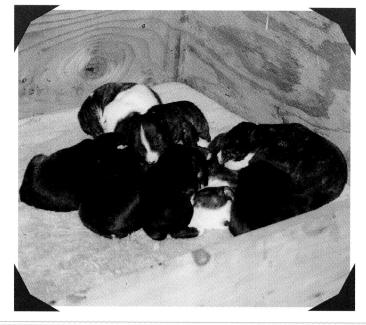

Litter of fat (and adorable) pups owned by Peter L. Colby of Newton's Junction, NH. Whelped 7/20/93 and sired by Colby's Grit.

Colby's Book of the

The Colby-bred bitch, Bandog Brittania, B, U-CD, SchH I, HC, WDS, winner of the highest title in weight pulling offered by the International Weight Pull Association, the "Working Dog Superior" or WDS. Britt, at 51 pounds, pulled 2,175 pounds for most pounds pulled per body weight at an IWPA-sanctioned pull. Britt also earned the HC, or "Herding Certification," which means she showed aptitude for stock work. The "B" is a German obedience-temperament test. The U-CD is an obedience title offered by the United Kennel Club, and the Schutzhund (SchH) I title includes following a human scent and indicating dropped articles such as wallets, complex off-leash obedience done in the presence of another dog, and police K-9 type bitework, where the dog must find and guard a "bad guy," stop him from escaping, and charge him from 50 yards away during the "courage test," biting and holding the bad guy until the owner arrives. Britt scored 97 out of 100 points for her "protection work," outscoring the other breeds. She remains, however, first and foremost a loving pet who adores children.

American Pit Bull Terrier

Below is a pedigree handwritten by J.P. Colby for his son Louis, of the dog "Blind Jack" whelped in 1932. This pedigree traces back to the most celebrated fighting dogs of English history, well into the past century. Louis recalls vividly that his father would sit by the fire in the evenings, talking dogs with his son, and reciting pedigrees from memory. How many other breeds sport such pedigrees, in fact, how many other breeds even existed in their present form when the dogs at the end of this pedigree were becoming champions? Not the German Shepherd, the Doberman, the Golden Retriever, nor most of the sporting and terrier breeds. Many breeds claim an ancient history but are sore-pressed to produce pictures and pedigrees such as this book contains. Due to show fads, most breeds have changed dramatically in the past several decades, often not even recognizable as the same dogs from which they came. Yet the Gas House Dog, Galvin's Pup, and Cockney Charlie's Pilot all could walk into the ring today and be competitive. The blood of those dogs surges through the Colby dogs of today, making them priceless living treasures. The preservation of the game-bred animals *must* be accomplished, even if they are to fight no more. They are a proud gift from the past, a gift that we may not all be able to appreciate, a gift that may only speak to the hearts of a few, but a gift

Opposite page: A rare poster advertising a fight convention from 1941. This poster is the only one of its kind in existence, and shows how openly dog fighting could be conducted earlier this century. This circular was mailed to J.P. by George Saddler (known as the "Mississippi Hawk"), one of the leading dog men in America. J.P. died six weeks prior to its arrival.

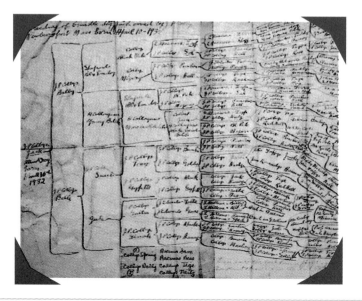

Handwritten pedigree of Blind Jack. This pedigree shows that all the Colby dogs were direct descendants of, as J.P. Colby clearly noted at the bottom fo the page, "the best fighting dogs in England and America in the last fifty years." Louis considers this pedigree one of his most treasured possessions.

The All-American Dog Convention Is On

Day after day, week after week, month after month, three fanciers, Earl Tudor, George Sadler, and Bob Hemphill have been working to bring together a full two days program of contests that will far surpass any convention ever held for pit dog men. Letter after letter, innumerable telegrams and long distance telephone calls were necessary to get this fine program arranged. Now the promotional work is done and I believe you will agree we have done a fine job.' We will have the best dogs in the country, you will see some expert handling and if you like to bet, you that were at the last one at Cleveland know you can get as little or as much covered as you care to bet. Here it is and we hope to see you there for the contests, the fun and the frolicking.

Place and Date

Cleveland, Miss., April 20-21. Two full days, Sunday and Monday. Headquarters will be at the Grover Hotel again, so come there when you arrive. We will have a headquarters suite of rooms for you to relax in and where you can see, talk, and listen to the Old Timers. In case you do not arrive until late, then you can get information at the following places: Hollowell's Cafe, Splendid Cafe, Delta Club, Sunrise Cafe on Hi-way 61, or telephone 502 or 127, and they will give you the information you want.

Where to Sleep

You can reserve a room at the Hotel or at one of the Tourist camps. Write or wire George Saddler for your reservations.

Bring Your Dogs

While we have a pretty full program of contests there will be time allotted for any fanciers who bring dogs and want to arrange pickup matches after you get there. If you are planning on bringing a dog for a pickup match then write Bob Hemphill, Summerville, S. C., and he will try and arrange a match for you in between the regularly scheduled contests. Then when you arrive at Cleveland with your dog get in touch with Hemphill at once so he can conclude the match and arrange the time on the program for you.

More Circulars

Be absolutely certain this circular does not get into the hands of anyone who is not in favor of contests. Do not talk or write to any one who is apt to report the convention. We had a wonderful time at Cleveland at the last one and everything is arranged for this one to go over smoothly, but WE MUST ALWAYS BE CAREFUL.

The Cost

The admittance cost will be $2.00 each day for men, $1.00 each day for ladies, and $1.00 each day for colored fanciers. Hotel and Tourist Camp rates are exceptionally reasonable.

The Program

Sunday, April 20th, Maxfield & Co., of New Orleans vs. Tudor & Company of Oklahoma. Male dogs at 34 lbs. top. Contest starts at 10:00 A. M.

Sunday, April 20, Bob Wallace and Crawford of Smackover, Ark., vs. Slim Emerson of Alabama. Male dogs at 42 lbs. top. Contests starts at 12:00 Noon.

Sunday, April 20th, Bisso & Co., of New Orleans vs. Hemphill & Co., of South Carolina. Dogs at 46 lbs. top. Contest starts at 2:00 P. M. This will bring together the famous Bob Tail of New Orleans and Golddust Gost.

Sunday, April 20th, Adair & Co., of Alabama vs. Saddler & Co., of Cleveland, Miss. Male dogs at 38 lbs. top. Contest starts at 4:00 P. M.

After this contest we will have exhibition rolls or any pickup fights. In between contests when we have a short one we will have pickup contests, exhibition rolls, and cock fights. Something will be going on ALL THE TIME.

Monday, April 21st, Hemphill & Co., of South Carolina vs. Saddler & Co., of Cleveland. Dogs at 40 lbs. t . Contest starts at 10 Noon. This will be between Solomon's Jax and Hemphill's Bashful Bully. Both of these dogs have won before.

Monday, April 21, Tudor & Company vs. Saddler & Co., male dogs at 47 lbs. top. Contest starts at 12 noon. Saddler's dog is the White Hope dog that won over Funderburg's Duke a short time ago.

Monday, April 21, Morris & Company of Kentucky vs. Trice & Company of Colorado. Females at 38 lbs. top. Contest starts at 2:00 P. M.

Monday, April 21, Trice & Co., of Colorado vs. Caudle & Co., of Summerville, S. C., male dogs 56 lbs., at 4:00 P. M.

There are several other matches in the making but not closed up as this goes to press. However, we will have one more money contest on the program Monday so you will see at least 8 money contests regularly scheduled during the convention. Once again —if you are bringing a dog or bitch for a pickup contest then write Hemphill at once and let him get busy and have someone bring a dog to go against you.

Now fellows this is our supreme effort to put on a convention that will afford action you see once in a life time. We have a wonderful place, absolute protection unless someone gets foolish and does too much talking. Everything is done openly, we have the freedom of the Hotels, Night Spots, and we can all have a wonderful time—Just be sure to keep the convention a topic to be discussed with DOG MEN ONLY.

We are printing some extra circulars and as before this mailing is being sent only to those who were on the mailing list the last time. If you have friends whom you know are okay, to whom you would like to send circulars, then write to George Saddler, Cleveland, Miss., Earl Tudor, Hobart, Okla., or Bob Hemphill, Summerville, S. C., and ask for as many circulars as you will need.

See you at Cleveland, Miss., April 20th to 21st.

George Saddler
Earl Tudor
Bob Hemphill

all the same. Man and dog alike, we share the past together, and the bold and sturdy fighting animals, the dog and the cock, appeal to those interested in preserving our past. And while the specter of a bull bait may not seem like a thing worth preserving, it is the matchless courage and sheer amazing heart of the dogs that were capable of such a feat that are worth saving. While there are several breeds of retrievers, sheepdogs, sled dogs, hounds, and police dogs, there has only been one dog that could bring a 2,000-pound bull to its knees, or fight four hours against an evenly matched opponent. No other dog will continue to do the task appointed to them by their master when exhausted beyond all measure, with broken limbs, torn flesh, ruined lungs. This is the legacy of the Pit Bull—the dog with the most heart.

Our ancestors—men like J.P. Colby—considered the dogs worth passing on to the future, and we can do no less. The challenge to today's breeder is to retain type, courage and gameness while producing a dog that can function in today's society. Some breeders, regardless of laws, will continue to

Colby's Nell and pup, circa 1973. Nell, out of Colby's Jill by Colby's Jesse, was the dam of many good and famous dogs such as Colby's Angus, Colby's Galtie II and Colby's Lotus.

Mo Vaughn, Boston Red Sox first baseman, with his Colby dog "Dexter" (UKC G728197, ADBA 64900E-53L). Mo, a "heavy hitter" both on and off the field (he helps raise funds for children who are desperately in need of operations) is proudly showing a first-place ribbon won by Dexter in a New England show.

measure their dogs by their ability to subdue other dogs. Others will test their dog's courage against pigs or bulls. The majority, however, will be challenged by finding modern legal means of testing their dogs.

Dogs of the Colby line are still being fought all over the world. Others are proving their worth through legal dog sports or work. Bandog Brittania, U-CD, B, HC, SchH I, WDS, a Colby-bred bitch, is an example of the Colby dogs adapting to today's world and tackling the work given them with the gameness of their ancestors. She is titled in the exacting sport of Schutzhund, has earned top honors and the highest award in weight-pulling contests, has earned obedience titles, is Herding Certified and was a registered therapy dog who made visitations to nursing homes to cheer elderly residents. A tough dog, she travelled all over North America with her owner for the Canine Aggression Research Center, working in seminars given to law enforcement, animal control and public utilities personnel on dog-related safety issues. In the steaming weather of Bermuda to the icy chill of Canada, she worked hard running officers through mock "attacks," often for hours at a time, and made thousands of friends for the breed. She is but one of many Colby-bred dogs working and playing all over the world today.

Colby treadmills designed for David Irwin.

The Colby family has been making dog treadmills for three generations now. The origin of the treadmill lies with the "turnspit" used to turn meat cooking over a fire. A small dog was placed on a small treadmill that was hooked up to a spit. As the dog walked the mill, the meat slowly turned, keeping it from scorching.

Louis states that his father was the first to make carpet mills. Carpet mills have a running surface made of carpet instead of wood slats. Louis made the treadmills for quite a while, and now his son Paul, who lives next door to Louis, continues the business.

Colby's Book of the

When the Polar explorer David Irwin was preparing his sled team for an Arctic journey, he asked J.P. to build him a special treadmill specifically for exercising a sled dog team! Irwin was preparing to make his historic crossing of 3,600 miles from Alaska to Hudson Bay. This was the longest trip alone by dog sled that anyone had made. The treadmill made for him by J.P. consisted of two separate treadmills, each wide enough to hold two huskies side-by-side. David Irwin gave this signed photo to the Colby family in thanks for their efforts.

David Irwin

A modern Colby treadmill, being modeled by a modern Colby dog!

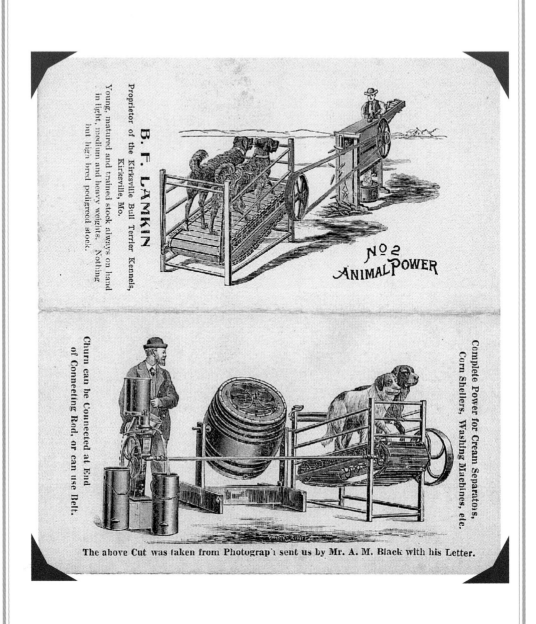

B. F. LAMKIN

Proprietor of the Kirksville Bull Terrier Kennels, Kirksville, Mo.

Young, matured and trained stock always on hand in light, medium and heavy weights. Nothing but high bred pedigreed stock.

NO 2 ANIMAL POWER

Complete Power for Cream Separators, Corn Shellers, Washing Machines, etc.

Churn can be Connected at End of Connecting Rod, or can use Belt.

The above Cut was taken from Photograph sent us by Mr. A. M. Black with his Letter.

An ad brochure circulated by B. F. Lamkin in the early 20th century. These treadmills were used for various purposes, including corn shelling, rotisserie cooking, and cream separating, to name a few.

Front cover of Lamkin brochure.

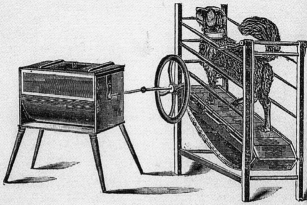

B. F. LAMKIN
Breeder of Dead Game Pit Bull Terriers.
General selling Agency for The Adjustable Patent.

ANIMAL POWERS.

No. 1.

Operated with

One Dog, Goat or Sheep,

Can be attached quickly and easily to

Churn, Fan Mill, Corn Sheller,

Pump, or Cream Separator,
Or Other Machines Requiring Light Power.

Turn of the century showing Irish Pyle cocks, which are ancestors of the Colby birds today.

Since the turn of the century the Colby family has also been associated with game fowl. J.P. had access to some of the original stock straight from England and Ireland, and developed several strains of worthy fighting birds. One of their strains, the Pyles, traces back to birds bred by Nathaniel Tracy and brought to Newburyport in the 1700s from Ireland. These birds are generally white or white and red and sport a long and proud history. Cocking was popular around the Boston area, and several breeds developed in and around the New England area. Another prestigious breed, still bred and valued today, is the Boston Roundhead. While cock

A photo from 36 Franklin Street. The building to the rear, with six windows, is one of the cock houses. It was very tall and the back wall had 20 coops, five to a row, four rows high. The top three rows were accessible only by ladder. The windows letting in the winter sun made it pleasant for the fowl, even if clean-up chores for a young Louis Colby were difficult!

Irish Pyle cock.

fighting is not legal in New England, it is legal in several states in the U.S., and the breeding of these birds is a huge business. Birds from the Colby strains are fighting and winning all over the world today.

While the Colby fowl no longer come blue/red, a reference to them from a 1928 issue of *Grit and Steel* magazine states, "among the good birds shown were three blue/red Gladiators from Colby, Newburyport, Massachusetts, all three winning." The blue/reds survive today in the breed called Old English Games and are popular in the Northeast.

Boston Roundhead ancestor, circa 1910.

A Colby Irish Pyle cock weighing 6 lbs. 8 oz. That is pretty big for a gamecock. Notice his comb, or the fleshy crest on his head and neck have been "dubbed," or removed. While this inhibits the bird's ability to dissipate heat, it does reduce the chance of bleeding to death, as the comb is a fleshy heat dissipation device filled with blood.

A "square-head" (straight comb) black/red cock that is two years old. This bird is a cross between an Irish Pyle and a Boston Roundhead. The cock has the straight comb of the Pyle, but the color of the Roundhead.

A view of the cozy coops that shelter Louis Colby's fowl during the harsh New England winters. Clear plastic lets in sun but cuts the wind. This happy Pyle cock holds court with his two wives.

Colby's Book of the

A beautiful Pyle cock with "something to crow about." A 5–pound, 6-ounce cock.

A handsome picture of a 5–pound, 8-ounce Boston Roundhead cock taken in May of 1993.

The game cock and the game Pit Bull may never appeal or be understood by a great many people. But one of the wonderful things about dogs is that there are so many different breeds that can appeal to so many different types of people. Just as one person may not be able to understand the love a person can have for a Pit Bull, neither can the Pit Bull owner understand the love a person could have for a cowardly, fear-biting, noisy little dog. It is not for people to judge the worth of each breed so long as there are people who value the dogs for their own sake. During the 1980s the Pit Bull suffered through a terrible bout of over-popularity with a resulting decrease in breed stability and popularity. It will be up to the breeders of the 21st century to stabilize the breed and maintain courage and

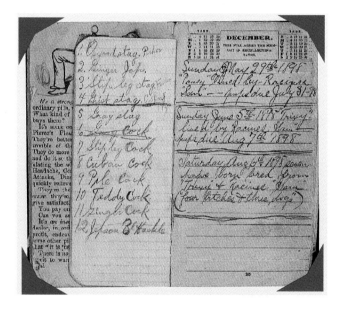

J.P. must have been preparing a show of cocks for a fight when he made this listing of birds in his notebook. Notice the date (1898) and the note of the breeding of three bitches to Racine's Sam.

heart with strong, functional bodies. The breed deserves to be respected and admired for its place in history, and on the merits of each individual dog. When one looks back upon the lifetimes of devotion given to the dogs by men like John P. and Louis Colby, one can see that these dogs often inspire the deepest devotion from their keepers.

A reprint from an 1887 circular showing the pit rules for cock fighting.

PIT RULES.

1st. All birds shall be weighed in the pit. Give or take two ounces.

2d. When a Stag is matched against a Cock or a Blinker against a sound bird, they shall be allowed four ounces the advantage.

3d. It shall be foul to sling blood or pull feathers, or clean beak. Either handler doing so shall lose the fight.

4th. Spurs may be cleaned.

5th. It shall be foul to touch birds while fighting, unless one is fast in the other; but if a cock should fasten himself with his own heels it shall be fair to handle, but under no other consideration.

6th. The handler may give a wing or turn his bird over when lying on its back.

7th. The longest liver, when both cocks are mortally wounded, shall be the winner.

8th. In counting, the bird showing fight last has the count.

9th. A fighting cock cannot break his own count.

10th. The handler having the count shall count 10, and pit his bird in his respective place and count 10 again and so on until he has counted 40. Then the birds must be placed breast to breast and he must count 40. When the battle is over, unless opposite bird shows fight by making a peck, wich breaks the count, and the fight proceeds.

11th. When time is called the handlers must let go their birds from their respective places, fair and square, fr it shall be foul for either handler to toss or sitch his bird upon his opponent's. For either violating the above rule shall lose the fight.

12th. Each party hall choose a judge, and the judges shall select a referee, who is a disinterested spectator. No person shall be competent to act as referee who has bet one cent, more or less, on the match or matches.

13th. It shall be the duty of the judges to watch the motions of the handlers, and if anything foul occurs they must appeal to the referee, whose decision shall be final. However, it will be the duty of the referee to notice all complaints from the judges alone and, after consideration, shall give his decision in strict accordance with these rules.

14th. The referee shall allow 30 seconds between each round, then call time. The handler failing or refusing to obey loses the fight.

15th. A cock running cannot win a fight; if both run they shall each be tried with a fresh cock. Should one show fight and the other not, the one showing fight shall be declared the winner. Should both refuse to show fight the battle shall be declared a draw.

16th. Any violation of the above rules loses the fight.

In conclusion, I would state that should you want any cocker's supplies such as muffs, knives, spurs, etc. I can furnish you with them. Two or three weeks' notice should be given for gaffs, as they are not carried in stock. They are worth from $5.00 to $7.50 per pair, any length or any pattern, made of very best material and of finest workmanship, and warranted to be just as represented.

Should you favor me with your orders for fowls or supplies I will please you or refund money. Correspondence from parties interested invited, which shall receive prompt attention.

Respectfully Yours,

JOHN L. EICHBERG,
BREEDER OF PIT GAMES EXCLUSIVELY,
Memphis, Tenn.

According to Louis, his father had no time for silly sentimental dog stories, and never read any. However, he did have one favorite piece of writing concerning a dog, Senator Vest's plea to the jury considering the case of a dog condemned to death. It is reproduced here as both J.P. and Louis feel it catches the very spirit of the American Pit Bull Terrier.

Louis Colby with Mo Vaughn of the Boston Red Sox with Colby's Dexter.

A PLEA TO THE JURY

"The best friend a man has in the world may turn against him, and become his enemy. His son or daughter that he has reared with loving care may prove ungrateful. Those who are nearest and dearest to us, those whom we trust with our happiness and our good name, may become traitor to their faith. The money that a man has he may lose. It flies away from him, perhaps when he needs it most. A man's reputation may be sacrificed in a moment of ill-considered action. The people who are prone to fall on their knees to do us honor when success is with us may be the first to throw the stone of malice when failure settles its cloud upon our heads.

"The one absolutely unselfish friend that a man can have in this world, the one that never deserts him, the one that never proves ungrateful or treacherous, is his dog. A man's dog stands by him in prosperity and in poverty, in health and in sickness. He will sleep on the cold ground, where the wintery winds blow and the snow drives fiercely, if only he may be near his master's side. He will kiss the hand that has no food to offer; he will lick the wounds that come in encounter with the roughness of the world. He guards the sleep of his pauper master as if he were a prince. When all other friends desert, he remains. When riches take wings, and reputation falls to pieces, he is as constant in his love as the sun in its journey through the heavens.

"If fortune drives the master forth an outcast in the world, friendless and homeless, the faithful dog asks no higher privilege than that of accompanying him, to guard him against danger, to fight his enemies. And when the last scene of all comes, and death takes his master, in its embrace, and his body is laid away in the cold ground, no matter if all other friends pursue their way, there by the graveside will the noble dog be found, his head between his paws, his eyes sad, but open in alert watchfulness, faithful and true even in death." Senator George Graham Vest (1830—1904).

SUGGESTED READING
Books on the American
Pit Bull Terrier

PS-613

176 pp,
120 photos.

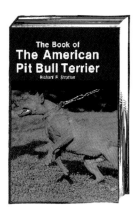

H-1024

352 pp,
68 color photos.

H-1063

288 pp,
104 color photos.

TS-142

320 pp,
Over 350
color photos

TS-235

320 pp,
Over 300
color photos.

TS-141

300 pp,
Ovr 300
color photos.

INDEX

Page numbers in **boldface** refer to illustrations.